STEPHEN BIESTY'S
INCREDIBLE
CROSS-SECTIONS
of EVERYTHING

ILLUSTRATED BY
STEPHEN BIESTY

WRITTEN BY
RICHARD PLATT

DK

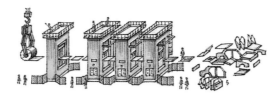

Penguin
Random
House

SECOND EDITION
Senior Editors Anna Streiffert Limerick, Ann Baggaley, Virien Chopra, Rupa Rao
Art Editor Chrissy Barnard
Managing Editors Francesca Baines, Kingshuk Ghoshal
Managing Art Editors Philip Letsu, Govind Mittal
US Editor Kayla Dugger **US Executive Editor** Lori Cates Hand
DTP Designers Pawan Kumar, Dheeraj Singh, Bimlesh Tiwary
Senior DTP Designer Sachin Singh
Pre-Production Manager Balwant Singh **Production Manager** Pankaj Sharma
Producer, Pre-Production Andy Hilliard **Production** Sian Cheung
Jacket Designer Akiko Kato **Jacket Editor** Emma Dawson
Jacket Design Development Manager Sophia MTT
Publisher Andrew Macintyre **Associate Publishing Director** Liz Wheeler
Art Director Karen Self **Publishing Director** Jonathan Metcalf

FIRST EDITION
Senior Art Editor Dorian Spencer Davies **Senior Editor** John C Miles
Deputy Art Director Miranda Kennedy **Deputy Editorial Director** Sophie Mitchell
Production Charlotte Traill **DTP Designer** Karen Nettelfield

This American Edition, 2020
First American Edition, 1997
Published in the United States by DK Publishing
1745 Broadway, 20th Floor, New York, NY 10019

Copyright © 1997, 2012, 2016, 2020 Dorling Kindersley Limited
DK, a Division of Penguin Random House LLC
24 25 10 9 8 7 6 5 4 3
008–316001–May/2020

A catalog record for this book is available from the Library of Congress.
ISBN 978-1-4654-9000-1

DK books are available at special discounts when purchased in bulk
for sales promotions, premiums, fund-raising, or educational use.
For details, contact: DK Publishing Special Markets,
1745 Broadway, 20th Floor, New York, NY 10019
SpecialSales@dk.com

Printed and bound in China

For the curious
www.dk.com

MIX
Paper | Supporting
responsible forestry
FSC™ C018179

This book was made with Forest
Stewardship Council™ certified
paper – one small step in DK's
commitment to a sustainable future.
For more information go to
www.dk.com/our-green-pledge

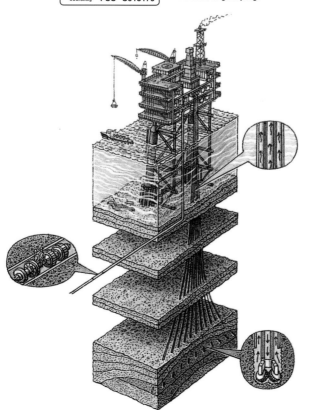

CONTENTS

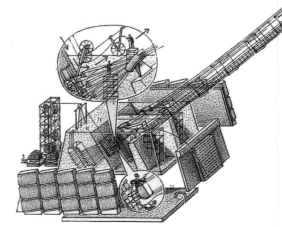

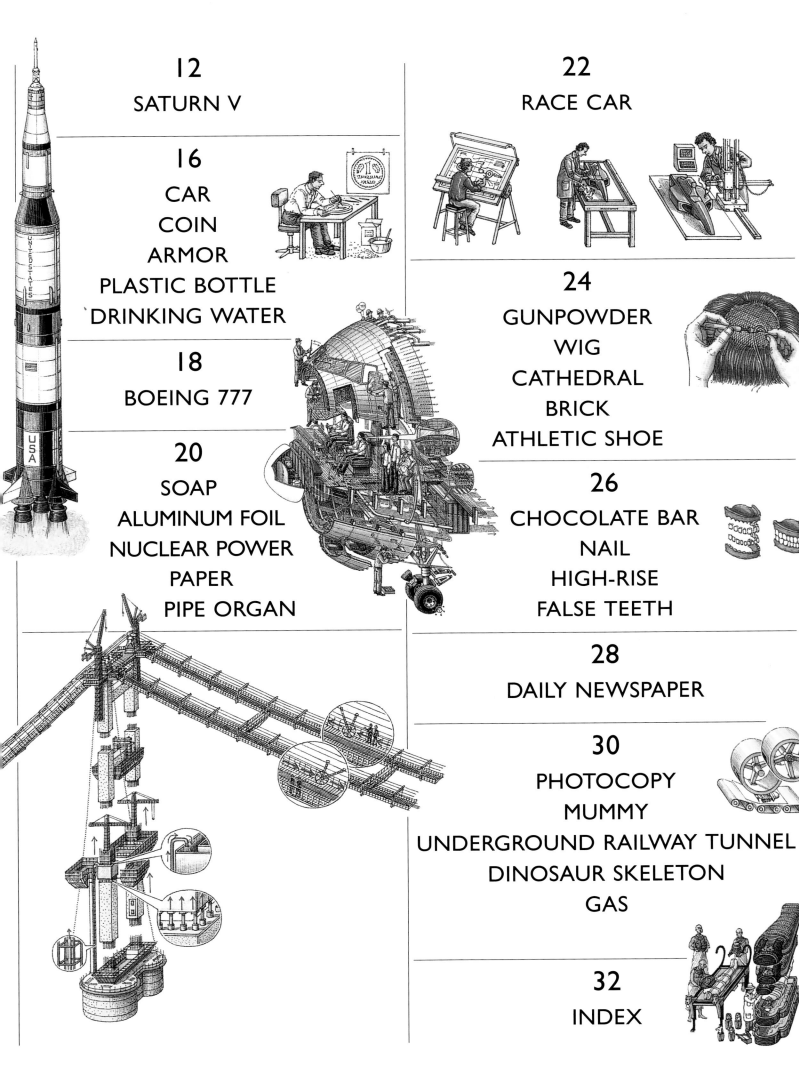

Our incredible world

"HELLO! I'M CHESTER THE TESTER. Stephen Biesty has asked me to help him find out how all sorts of fascinating things are made. Some are everyday objects, such as a newspaper; others are amazing creations, like a rocket that can take humans to the moon. Checking everything thoroughly is serious work—do you have any idea how much testing needs to be done in a chocolate factory? But my assistant, Hector the inspector, is going to help—so look out for us at work."

"Chester, would you mind testing my sandwiches? I'm not sure which are the peanut butter and jelly ones!"

"Now, let's see how fast this monster can move."

Model dinosaur

"Aiieee, careful! These swords are really sharp."

Armor

Race car

"This string seems strong enough to me."

Nuclear power station

Plywood

High-rise

"Have you seen my mummy?"

Gunpowder

"The gunpowder testing is very noisy, so I'm wearing my earplugs."

"Incredible! The cannon still works after all these years."

Steam locomotive

"I wonder what happens here?"

"It's not often I get to travel in this manner!"

Gas

Drinking water

Underground railway tunnel

Newspaper

Bric

"This beats the crush inside."

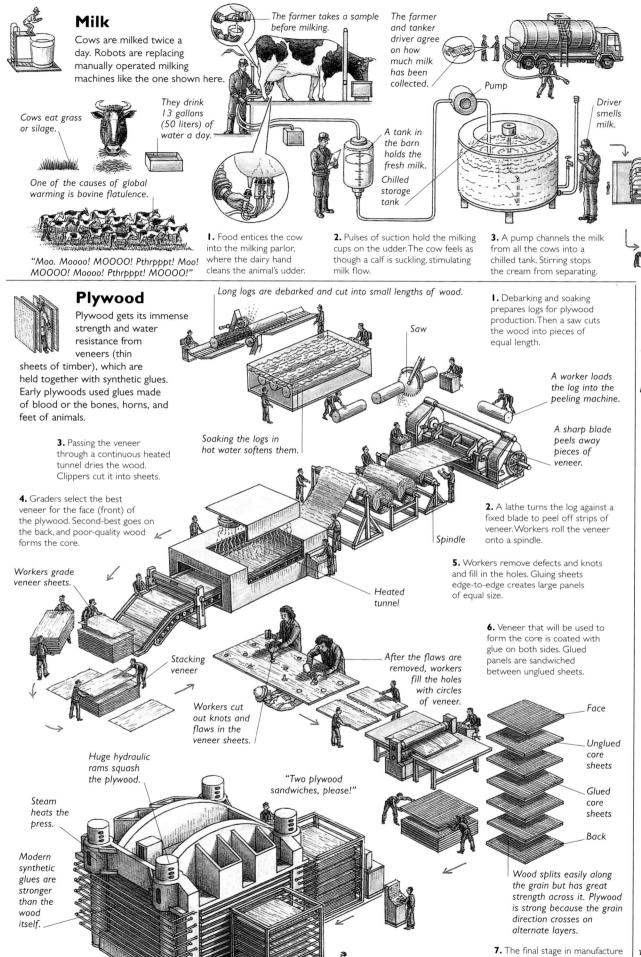

Milk

Cows are milked twice a day. Robots are replacing manually operated milking machines like the one shown here.

Cows eat grass or silage.

They drink 13 gallons (50 liters) of water a day.

One of the causes of global warming is bovine flatulence.

"Moo. Moooo! MOOOO! Pthrpppt! Moo! MOOOO! Moooo! Pthrpppt! MOOOO!"

The farmer takes a sample before milking.

The farmer and tanker driver agree on how much milk has been collected.

Pump

A tank in the barn holds the fresh milk. Chilled storage tank

Driver smells milk.

4. A tanker collects the day's milk. The driver smells it before pumping it up.

5. A truck scale (drive-on scale) at the dairy measures the weight of the tanker to check the quantity of milk.

The tanker drives on full …

… and drives off unloaded.

1. Food entices the cow into the milking parlor, where the dairy hand cleans the animal's udder.

2. Pulses of suction hold the milking cups on the udder. The cow feels as though a calf is suckling, stimulating milk flow.

3. A pump channels the milk from all the cows into a chilled tank. Stirring stops the cream from separating.

Milk is pumped to the dairy's bulk reservoir.

Plywood

Plywood gets its immense strength and water resistance from veneers (thin sheets of timber), which are held together with synthetic glues. Early plywoods used glues made of blood or the bones, horns, and feet of animals.

3. Passing the veneer through a continuous heated tunnel dries the wood. Clippers cut it into sheets.

4. Graders select the best veneer for the face (front) of the plywood. Second-best goes on the back, and poor-quality wood forms the core.

Workers grade veneer sheets.

Long logs are debarked and cut into small lengths of wood.

Saw

1. Debarking and soaking prepares logs for plywood production. Then a saw cuts the wood into pieces of equal length.

A worker loads the log into the peeling machine.

A sharp blade peels away pieces of veneer.

Soaking the logs in hot water softens them.

2. A lathe turns the log against a fixed blade to peel off strips of veneer. Workers roll the veneer onto a spindle.

Spindle

5. Workers remove defects and knots and fill in the holes. Gluing sheets edge-to-edge creates large panels of equal size.

Heated tunnel

Stacking veneer

After the flaws are removed, workers fill the holes with circles of veneer.

6. Veneer that will be used to form the core is coated with glue on both sides. Glued panels are sandwiched between unglued sheets.

Workers cut out knots and flaws in the veneer sheets.

Face

Unglued core sheets

Glued core sheets

Back

Huge hydraulic rams squash the plywood.

"Two plywood sandwiches, please!"

Steam heats the press.

Modern synthetic glues are stronger than the wood itself.

Wood splits easily along the grain but has great strength across it. Plywood is strong because the grain direction crosses on alternate layers.

7. The final stage in manufacture is to bond the plywood together. A gigantic press squeezes and heats stacks of assembled veneer "sandwiches."

Finished sheets are removed from the press and stacked.

Wooden house

Many houses built since about 1835 are constructed using a lightweight frame, with strips of thin timber in place of the heavy timbers used in older houses.

Damp-proof course

1. The house stands on solid foundations made by digging trenches and filling them with concrete. A damp-proof course (a strip of waterproof material) keeps the wall above it dry.

On houses such as this one, the finished frame is clad with wood. Other houses may have brick or flat pieces of stone as cladding.

The carpenters' fashion for exposing thin wooden supports led people to nickname homes like these "stick-style" houses.

This style of wooden house became fashionable as cities spread out into suburbs a century ago.

Details such as this gable trim are made elsewhere.

6. A dairy technician checks the milk before pumping it out of the tanker and into one of the bulk reservoirs.

7. A separator skims off the lighter, fattier cream from the rest of the milk. The cream will make cheese or butter—or go straight onto apple pie!

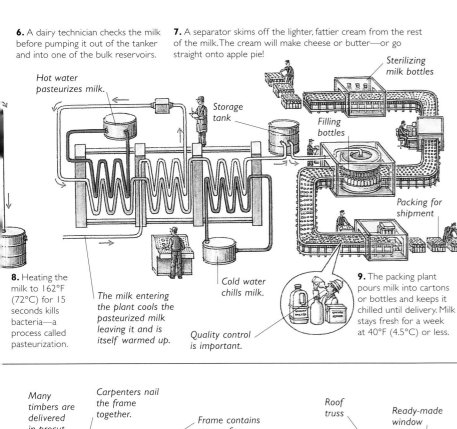

Hot water pasteurizes milk.

Storage tank

Sterilizing milk bottles

Filling bottles

Packing for shipment

8. Heating the milk to 162°F (72°C) for 15 seconds kills bacteria—a process called pasteurization.

The milk entering the plant cools the pasteurized milk leaving it and is itself warmed up.

Cold water chills milk.

Quality control is important.

9. The packing plant pours milk into cartons or bottles and keeps it chilled until delivery. Milk stays fresh for a week at 40°F (4.5°C) or less.

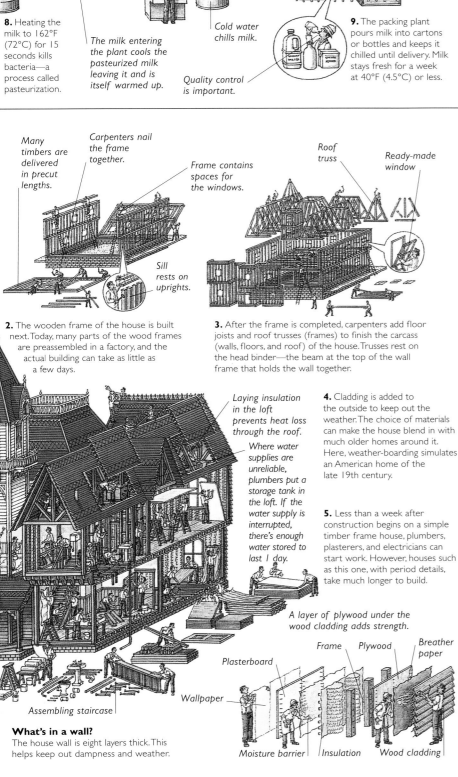

Many timbers are delivered in precut lengths.

Carpenters nail the frame together.

Frame contains spaces for the windows.

Roof truss

Ready-made window

Sill rests on uprights.

2. The wooden frame of the house is built next. Today, many parts of the wood frames are preassembled in a factory, and the actual building can take as little as a few days.

3. After the frame is completed, carpenters add floor joists and roof trusses (frames) to finish the carcass (walls, floors, and roof) of the house. Trusses rest on the head binder—the beam at the top of the wall frame that holds the wall together.

Laying insulation in the loft prevents heat loss through the roof.

Where water supplies are unreliable, plumbers put a storage tank in the loft. If the water supply is interrupted, there's enough water stored to last 1 day.

4. Cladding is added to the outside to keep out the weather. The choice of materials can make the house blend in with much older homes around it. Here, weather-boarding simulates an American home of the late 19th century.

5. Less than a week after construction begins on a simple timber frame house, plumbers, plasterers, and electricians can start work. However, houses such as this one, with period details, take much longer to build.

A layer of plywood under the wood cladding adds strength.

Assembling staircase

What's in a wall?
The house wall is eight layers thick. This helps keep out dampness and weather.

Plasterboard *Frame* *Plywood* *Breather paper*
Wallpaper *Moisture barrier* *Insulation* *Wood cladding*

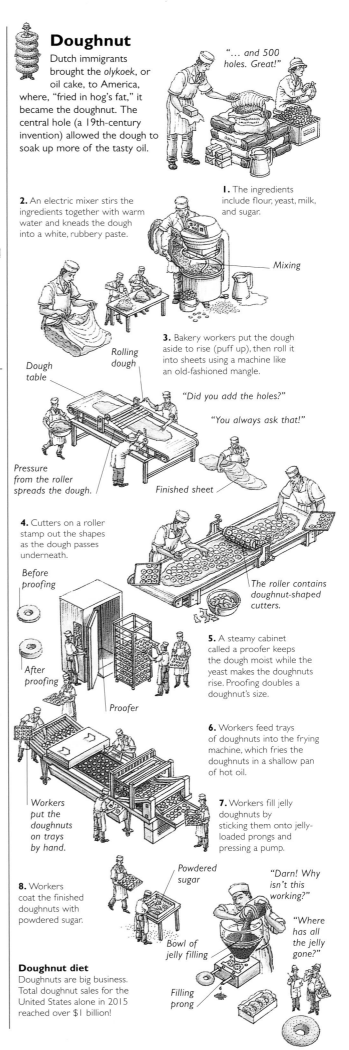

Doughnut

Dutch immigrants brought the *olykoek*, or oil cake, to America, where, "fried in hog's fat," it became the doughnut. The central hole (a 19th-century invention) allowed the dough to soak up more of the tasty oil.

"... and 500 holes. Great!"

1. The ingredients include flour, yeast, milk, and sugar.

2. An electric mixer stirs the ingredients together with warm water and kneads the dough into a white, rubbery paste.

Mixing

3. Bakery workers put the dough aside to rise (puff up), then roll it into sheets using a machine like an old-fashioned mangle.

Dough table *Rolling dough*

"Did you add the holes?"

"You always ask that!"

Pressure from the roller spreads the dough. *Finished sheet*

4. Cutters on a roller stamp out the shapes as the dough passes underneath.

Before proofing

The roller contains doughnut-shaped cutters.

After proofing

Proofer

5. A steamy cabinet called a proofer keeps the dough moist while the yeast makes the doughnuts rise. Proofing doubles a doughnut's size.

6. Workers feed trays of doughnuts into the frying machine, which fries the doughnuts in a shallow pan of hot oil.

7. Workers fill jelly doughnuts by sticking them onto jelly-loaded prongs and pressing a pump.

Workers put the doughnuts on trays by hand.

Powdered sugar

"Darn! Why isn't this working?"

"Where has all the jelly gone?"

8. Workers coat the finished doughnuts with powdered sugar.

Bowl of jelly filling

Filling prong

Doughnut diet
Doughnuts are big business. Total doughnut sales for the United States alone in 2015 reached over $1 billion!

CD (Compact disc)

A compact disc can store up to 80 minutes of music, or more than 100 million words—the equivalent of almost 500 books.

Washing *Coating* *Oven drying*

1. Washed glass discs are coated with a special solution and dried. This prepares the surface for the laser "cutting" machine.

Digitally recorded music is converted to a laser signal.

2. Music recorded digitally (as on-off signals) controls a laser, which burns a series of tiny dots on the disc surface.

Developing

Production workers dress like surgeons to keep dust from marring the discs.

3. Developing fluid etches the burned areas, forming pits. Electroforming follows. This deposits nickel on the glass master.

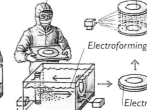

The metal layer is separated from the glass master.

Electroforming

"Father" *"Mother"* *"Son"*

"Mother"

Electroformed master

4. The metal layer ("father") has a negative impression. It is used to create several positives ("mothers").

Steam locomotive

Locomotives powered by steam once hauled every train. Heat from a coal fire in the locomotive's firebox boiled water in the boiler to create steam. The pressurized steam then pushed on pistons contained within the locomotive's cylinders. This power drove the wheels via metal connecting rods. Some locomotives covered three times the distance to the moon and back in their working lives. Locomotive factories built them from scratch: raw materials went in one gate, and completed locomotives steamed out of another.

Foundry workers made by hand the molds used for casting.

Workers unpack a casting.

Pouring molten metal

Finished casting

A narrow-gauge railway moved heavy objects within the works.

Steam hammer

The machined cylinder block moved to the next stage.

1. The first step was to cast the cylinder blocks. Workers packed sand around wooden patterns to create half-molds. They then removed the patterns and united the halves. Pouring in hot iron created a complete casting.

2. In the metalworking shop, smiths machined the castings precisely and hammered other parts into shape using a huge steam-powered hammer. The sound of the steam hammer traveled a long way.

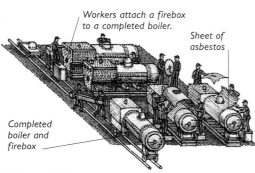

Workers attach a firebox to a completed boiler.

Sheet of asbestos

Completed boiler and firebox

5. After the boiler was assembled, it was attached to the firebox, where coal was burned to turn water into steam. Then the boiler was insulated with sheets of asbestos (mineral fiber) to prevent heat loss.

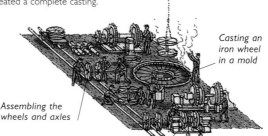

Casting an iron wheel in a mold

Assembling the wheels and axles

Giant lathe

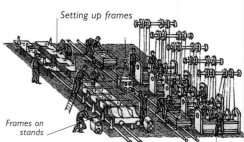

Setting up frames

Frames on stands

The lathes were belt-driven from a central source.

---

6. The locomotive rolled along on cast-iron wheels. These were cast next. Steel tires were fitted onto the wheels to make a tough, wear-resistant rim. Boys as young as 13 shaped the wheels on giant lathes.

7. In the erecting shop, workers assembled the frames. Until the wheels were completed, the frames rested on cone-shaped stands. Other workers machined precision parts on lathes.

Matches

Friction matches were invented by British chemist John Walker in 1827. Before this date, tinderboxes were used to make fire. A spark was made by striking a flint, lighting the tinder in the box.

Cutting to length *Blade peels veneer*

Sheet of veneer

Close-up of splints

1. Logs arrive at the factory and are cut to length. A machine then peels off veneer—thin sheets of wood.

2. Stacks of veneer are sliced into "splints" by a giant blade, making about 2 million every hour.

5. The match-making machine is the size of two double-decker buses. An endless belt winds through it. The belt grips the matches at one end and carries them through the machine.

6. To make the match burn fiercely once it has ignited, each splint passes through a trough of paraffin wax. The path of the belt ensures that only the tips are coated.

Finished splints

A belt holds the matches in neat rows.

Splints are fed into a blower to go to the match-making machine.

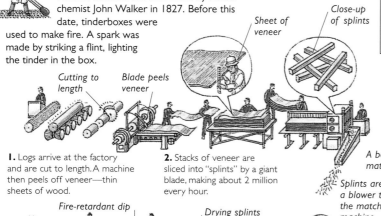

Fire-retardant dip

Drying splints

3. Sifting removes splints that are the wrong size. A dip in fire-retardant liquid ensures that they don't smolder after use.

4. The splints are dried, then tumbled in a drum to smooth them. They are then blown along tubes to the match-making machine.

The match head is dipped in a chemical mixture.

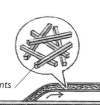
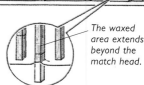

The waxed area extends beyond the match head.

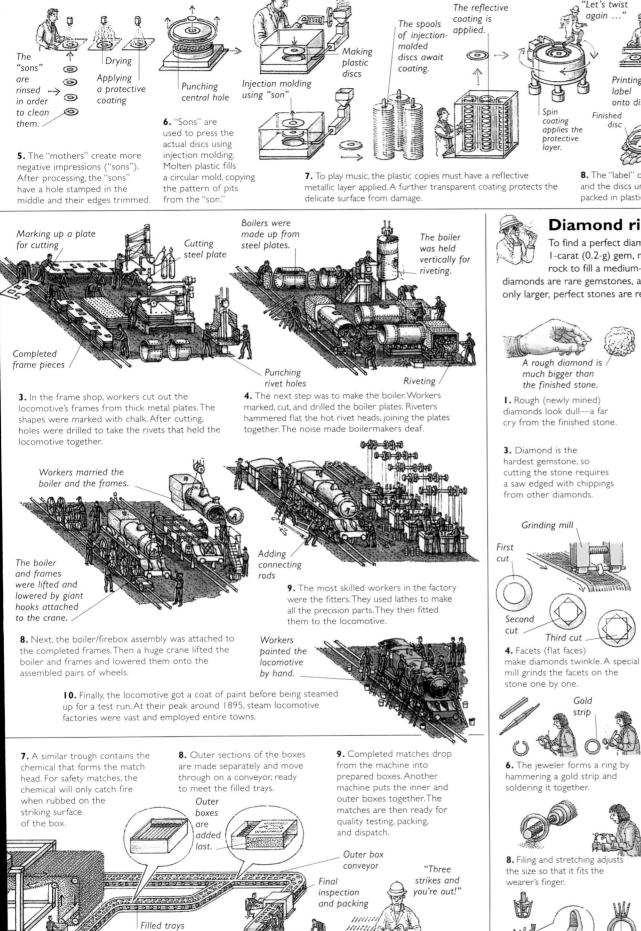

The "sons" are rinsed → in order to clean them.

Drying

Applying a protective coating

Punching central hole

Injection molding using "son"

Making plastic discs

The spools of injection-molded discs await coating.

The reflective coating is applied.

"Let's twist again ..."

Final checking

Printing label onto disc

Finished disc

Spin coating applies the protective layer.

5. The "mothers" create more negative impressions ("sons"). After processing, the "sons" have a hole stamped in the middle and their edges trimmed.

6. "Sons" are used to press the actual discs using injection molding. Molten plastic fills a circular mold, copying the pattern of pits from the "son."

7. To play music, the plastic copies must have a reflective metallic layer applied. A further transparent coating protects the delicate surface from damage.

8. The "label" on the back of the disc is printed on, and the discs undergo final checks before being packed in plastic "jewel cases."

Marking up a plate for cutting

Cutting steel plate

Completed frame pieces

Punching rivet holes

Boilers were made up from steel plates.

The boiler was held vertically for riveting.

Riveting

3. In the frame shop, workers cut out the locomotive's frames from thick metal plates. The shapes were marked with chalk. After cutting, holes were drilled to take the rivets that held the locomotive together.

4. The next step was to make the boiler. Workers marked, cut, and drilled the boiler plates. Riveters hammered flat the hot rivet heads, joining the plates together. The noise made boilermakers deaf.

Workers married the boiler and the frames.

The boiler and frames were lifted and lowered by giant hooks attached to the crane.

Adding connecting rods

9. The most skilled workers in the factory were the fitters. They used lathes to make all the precision parts. They then fitted them to the locomotive.

Workers painted the locomotive by hand.

8. Next, the boiler/firebox assembly was attached to the completed frames. Then a huge crane lifted the boiler and frames and lowered them onto the assembled pairs of wheels.

10. Finally, the locomotive got a coat of paint before being steamed up for a test run. At their peak around 1895, steam locomotive factories were vast and employed entire towns.

---

7. A similar trough contains the chemical that forms the match head. For safety matches, the chemical will only catch fire when rubbed on the striking surface of the box.

8. Outer sections of the boxes are made separately and move through on a conveyor, ready to meet the filled trays.

Outer boxes are added last.

9. Completed matches drop from the machine into prepared boxes. Another machine puts the inner and outer boxes together. The matches are then ready for quality testing, packing, and dispatch.

Outer box conveyor

"Three strikes and you're out!"

Final inspection and packing

Filled trays

The matches fit into slots in the endless belt.

A hard life
A century ago, children made matches by hand. A match girl's daily wages wouldn't even buy one box today.

Diamond ring

To find a perfect diamond big enough to cut into a 1-carat (0.2-g) gem, miners may have to dig out enough rock to fill a medium-sized apartment building. Although diamonds are rare gemstones, advertising exaggerates their value; only larger, perfect stones are really precious.

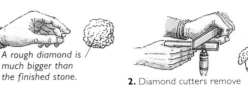

A rough diamond is much bigger than the finished stone.

Split stone

1. Rough (newly mined) diamonds look dull—a far cry from the finished stone.

2. Diamond cutters remove imperfections by cleaving the stone along its natural grain.

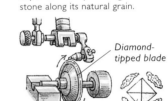

3. Diamond is the hardest gemstone, so cutting the stone requires a saw edged with chippings from other diamonds.

Diamond-tipped blade

The saw cuts the stone into a recognizable shape.

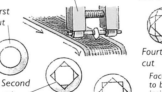

Grinding mill

First cut

Second cut

Third cut

Fourth cut

Fifth cut

Sixth cut

Facets allow the light to bounce around inside the stone.

4. Facets (flat faces) make diamonds twinkle. A special mill grinds the facets on the stone one by one.

5. The 58 facets of a "brilliant" diamond are made by repeatedly grinding and polishing the stone.

Gold strip

Mandrel

6. The jeweler forms a ring by hammering a gold strip and soldering it together.

7. Gently hammering the ring on a mandrel (a round anvil) shapes it into a precise circle.

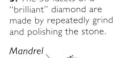

8. Filing and stretching adjusts the size so that it fits the wearer's finger.

9. The jeweler makes the setting by cutting the shape and bending the prongs to grip the stone.

The prong holds the stone in place when bent over.

Finished setting

Mounting the diamond lets light in underneath so that the stone sparkles.

Finished ring

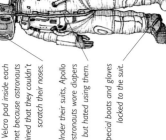

the Lun...

Lift-off!
The picture above shows how the three stages of the rocket and the sections of the spacecraft fitted together.

Building the Lunar Module
The Lunar Module was made up of two parts. The descent stage took the craft from the orbiting Command Module to the moon, where it was left behind. Meanwhile, the astronauts returned to the Command Module in the ascent stage.

In the moon's thin atmosphere, the Lunar Module did not need to be streamlined and had an angular, buglike shape.

Spring thrusters helped remove the panels of the adapter.

During launch, this adapter protected the Lunar Module and held the Command and Service Modules in place. When the spacecraft left Earth orbit, the adapter's panels opened like flower petals.

Layers of nickel, aluminum, and reflective Mylar protected the outside of the Lunar Module from the Sun's heat. The Mylar was carefully hand-crumpled before installation to improve its insulating qualities.

Technicians pasted a scratchy Velcro pad inside each helmet because astronauts complained that they couldn't scratch their noses.

Under their suits, Apollo astronauts wore diapers but hated using them.

Special boots and gloves locked to the suit.

5. Each of the first five EMUs cost $1 million. They were constantly improved until they allowed complete freedom and were comfortable enough to wear for up to 7 hours.

Instrument unit
At the top of the third stage, the Instrument Unit housed the "brains" of Saturn V. IBM computers steered the rocket motors, ensuring that the spacecraft traveled into the correct orbit. In case of breakdown, each computer had three twin "sisters" that could take over.

Perhaps the most important instrument was an inertial guidance system—a gyroscope that sensed the slightest movement. If the launch vehicle tilted slightly, the inertial guidance system would send instructions to turn the rocket motors, steering it back on course.

Third stage
The third and smallest stage of the Saturn V launcher was the only one to reach Earth orbit. After circling Earth once or twice, the astronauts fired its engine for the last time to blast their craft toward the moon. Its work complete, the discarded third stage became just another piece of space junk.

Thermal tiles 1.5 in (37 mm) thick kept the contents of the liquid oxygen and hydrogen tanks ultra-cold. The tiles were so effective that if ice had filled one of these tanks, it would have taken 12 years to reach room temperature.

The liquid hydrogen fuel was stored at -423°F (-252°C).

Inside all the tanks, there were structures called baffles to stop the contents from sloshing around.

A service tunnel carried power and control cables along the exterior. More than 2,500,000 soldered joints linked these cables.

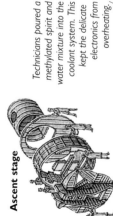

Eight spheres contained high-pressure helium gas, which forced LOX into the engines.

A umbilical connector carried data to the ground while the rocket stood on its launch pad.

Liquid oxygen (LOX) tank

Stage separation system

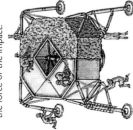

Descent stage
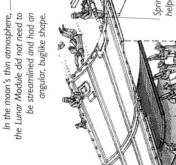

1. Construction of the descent stage began with the aluminum frames that supported the engine, fuel, and oxidizer tanks.

2. A honeycomb material filled the buglike legs. Touchdown crushed the honeycomb, absorbing the force of the impact.

3. Technicians installed the pipework and wrapped the descent stage in its "cooking-foil" blanket.

Ascent stage
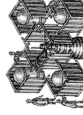

Technicians poured a methylated spirit and water mixture into the coolant system. This kept the delicate electronics from overheating.

1. The ascent stage was the "cab" in which the crew would travel. Engineers welded and bolted it together from carefully milled aluminum subassemblies.

2. When the ascent-stage structure was complete, assembly continued in a clean room, where engineers installed life support, propulsion, and navigation subsystems.

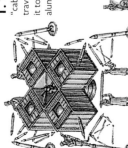

3. A thin aluminum skin covered the protective thermal blanket of the ascent stage to protect crew and equipment from micrometeorites.

Saturn V

WHEN THE AMERICAN SPACE PROGRAM FINALLY achieved a moon landing on July 20, 1969, the Apollo 11 spacecraft was launched by a powerful rocket called Saturn V. The most powerful rocket ever, Saturn V was used to launch all the Apollo spacecraft on lunar missions. The rocket alone stood 363 feet (110 meters) high and had three stages, each of which fell away when it ran out of fuel. To follow what happened as Saturn V took off, start at the first stage at the bottom right of the page.

Command Module

During their journey to the moon, the astronauts lived in the Command Module. While two of them descended to the lunar surface, the third stayed behind in the orbiting craft. Building this capsule was perhaps the most complex task of the Apollo program: it had over 2 million parts. (A car has around 2,000.)

1. The pressurized crew compartment was only a little larger than a compact car, but in this small space, the astronauts had to eat, sleep, work, and keep clean for over a week.

2. Special shields surrounded the Command Module to protect it from the intense heat generated by reentering Earth's atmosphere. The Command Module fell through the atmosphere until it was 24,000 ft (7,300 m) above the ocean. Then small "drogue" parachutes opened to slow the descent. The main parachutes opened later, slowing the craft enough to splash into the ocean safely.

Escape tower

If the Saturn rocket caught fire on the ground or during launch, motors in the escape tower would ignite. The tower would then carry the Command Module clear of the launch site and just high enough for its parachutes to open and slow its descent.

The crew crawled into the Lunar Module through this access tunnel.

The Lunar Module linked up to the Command Module at the docking ring.

Nearly 250 nylon strands held the capsule to the landing parachutes.

The heat shield was made up of seven different layers.

Drogue parachute

The rocket motor had the power of 4,300 cars.

Escape tower

Lunar Module pilot

Command Module pilot

Service Module

Secured to the base of the Command Module, the tubular Service Module carried supplies of fuel and oxidizer, plus water and oxygen for the crew. Its rocket motor moved the spacecraft into lunar orbit and powered it back to Earth.

The flight computer had only 32K of memory—today's home computers have 100 times as much.

The Mission Commander and the other astronauts wore their suits during the launch, but later slipped into something more comfortable.

Small jets were positioned all around the spacecraft. Controlling the firing of these rockets enabled the astronauts to turn the craft.

Service Module engine

The filling in the honeycomb structure of the walls cooled the craft.

Engine nozzle

Lunar Module

The Lunar Module was the only part of the Apollo 11 mission to land on the moon. On launch, the Lunar Module was secured below the Command and Service Modules (CSM). Once out of Earth orbit, the petal-like doors protecting the Lunar Module fell away. The crew then separated the CSM, turned it upside down, and linked up with the exposed Lunar Module. Finally, springs separated the Lunar Module from the third stage.

Antennae for transmitting and receiving information from mission control

Escape tower
Command Module
Service Module
Section housing Lunar Module
Instrument unit
Third stage
Interstage ring

Apollo spacecraft

Second stage

Interstage ring

First stage

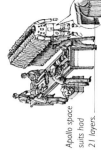

Apollo space suits had 21 layers.

Space suit

On the moon, Extravehicular Mobility Units (EMUs or space suits) protected astronauts from the vacuum of space and from heat, cold, radiation, and meteors. Each astronaut had three tailor-made EMUs: one mission suit, one training suit, and one backup suit.

1. The fabrics were high-tech, but the construction process was conventional, and expert workers sewed the seams.

2. The EMU was actually three garments: liquid-cooled underwear, a pressurized suit, and a protective cover.

Small tubes were sewn into the fabric of the underwear.

3. To reduce sweating, cool water circulated through small tubes running through the all-in-one underwear. Sweat was not only uncomfortable, it also misted the helmet visor, blocking vision.

4. Hoses at chest level carried oxygen from the suit through the Portable Life Support System (PLSS), which filtered it to remove carbon dioxide, flatulence, and moisture from sweat.

Bridge

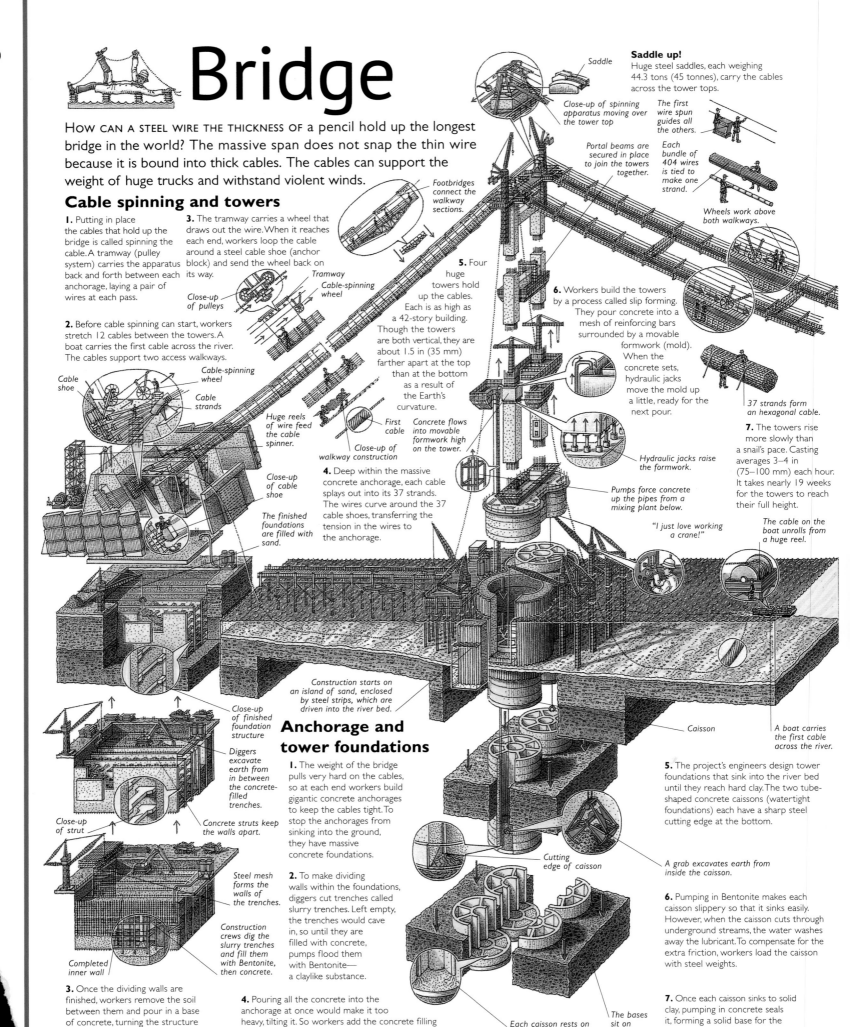

HOW CAN A STEEL WIRE THE THICKNESS OF a pencil hold up the longest bridge in the world? The massive span does not snap the thin wire because it is bound into thick cables. The cables can support the weight of huge trucks and withstand violent winds.

Cable spinning and towers

1. Putting in place the cables that hold up the bridge is called spinning the cable. A tramway (pulley system) carries the apparatus back and forth between each anchorage, laying a pair of wires at each pass.

2. Before cable spinning can start, workers stretch 12 cables between the towers. A boat carries the first cable across the river. The cables support two access walkways.

3. The tramway carries a wheel that draws out the wire. When it reaches each end, workers loop the cable around a steel cable shoe (anchor block) and send the wheel back on its way.

4. Deep within the massive concrete anchorage, each cable splays out into its 37 strands. The wires curve around the 37 cable shoes, transferring the tension in the wires to the anchorage.

5. Four huge towers hold up the cables. Each is as high as a 42-story building. Though the towers are both vertical, they are about 1.5 in (35 mm) farther apart at the top than at the bottom as a result of the Earth's curvature.

6. Workers build the towers by a process called slip forming. They pour concrete into a mesh of reinforcing bars surrounded by a movable formwork (mold). When the concrete sets, hydraulic jacks move the mold up a little, ready for the next pour.

7. The towers rise more slowly than a snail's pace. Casting averages 3–4 in (75–100 mm) each hour. It takes nearly 19 weeks for the towers to reach their full height.

Labels (Cable spinning and towers)

- Footbridges connect the walkway sections.
- Tramway
- Cable-spinning wheel
- Close-up of pulleys
- Cable shoe
- Cable-spinning wheel
- Cable strands
- Huge reels of wire feed the cable spinner.
- Close-up of cable shoe
- The finished foundations are filled with sand.
- First cable
- Close-up of walkway construction
- Concrete flows into movable formwork high on the tower.
- Hydraulic jacks raise the formwork.
- Pumps force concrete up the pipes from a mixing plant below.
- "I just love working a crane!"
- The cable on the boat unrolls from a huge reel.
- Saddle
- Close-up of spinning apparatus moving over the tower top
- Portal beams are secured in place to join the towers together.

Saddle up!
Huge steel saddles, each weighing 44.3 tons (45 tonnes), carry the cables across the tower tops.

- The first wire spun guides all the others.
- Each bundle of 404 wires is tied to make one strand.
- Wheels work above both walkways.
- 37 strands form an hexagonal cable.

Anchorage and tower foundations

1. The weight of the bridge pulls very hard on the cables, so at each end workers build gigantic concrete anchorages to keep the cables tight. To stop the anchorages from sinking into the ground, they have massive concrete foundations.

2. To make dividing walls within the foundations, diggers cut trenches called slurry trenches. Left empty, the trenches would cave in, so until they are filled with concrete, pumps flood them with Bentonite—a claylike substance.

3. Once the dividing walls are finished, workers remove the soil between them and pour in a base of concrete, turning the structure into a huge partitioned box.

4. Pouring all the concrete into the anchorage at once would make it too heavy, tilting it. So workers add the concrete filling gradually, balancing the increasing tension in the cable.

5. The project's engineers design tower foundations that sink into the river bed until they reach hard clay. The two tube-shaped concrete caissons (watertight foundations) each have a sharp steel cutting edge at the bottom.

6. Pumping in Bentonite makes each caisson slippery so that it sinks easily. However, when the caisson cuts through underground streams, the water washes away the lubricant. To compensate for the extra friction, workers load the caisson with steel weights.

7. Once each caisson sinks to solid clay, pumping in concrete seals it, forming a solid base for the construction of the huge towers.

Labels (Anchorage and tower foundations)

- Close-up of finished foundation structure
- Diggers excavate earth from in between the concrete-filled trenches.
- Close-up of strut
- Concrete struts keep the walls apart.
- Steel mesh forms the walls of the trenches.
- Construction crews dig the slurry trenches and fill them with Bentonite, then concrete.
- Completed inner wall
- Construction starts on an island of sand, enclosed by steel strips, which are driven into the river bed.
- Caisson
- A boat carries the first cable across the river.
- A grab excavates earth from inside the caisson.
- Cutting edge of caisson
- Each caisson rests on a concrete base plug.
- The bases sit on solid clay.

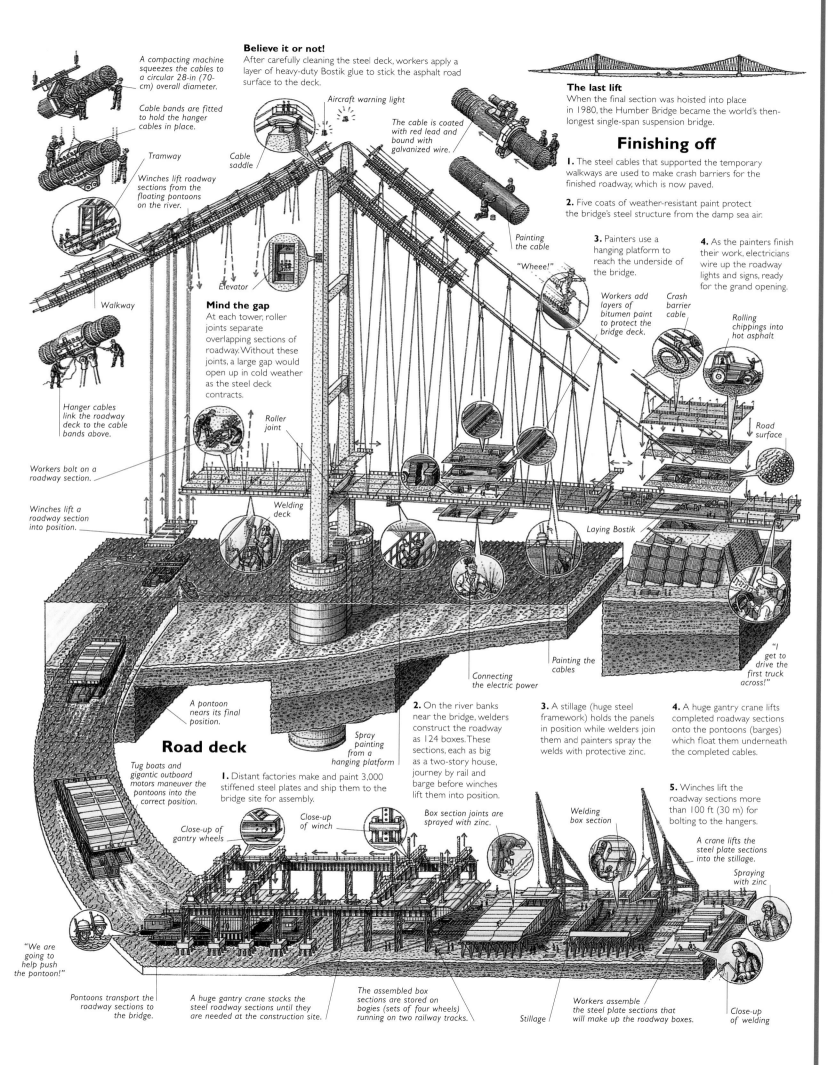

A compacting machine squeezes the cables to a circular 28-in (70-cm) overall diameter.

Cable bands are fitted to hold the hanger cables in place.

Tramway

Winches lift roadway sections from the floating pontoons on the river.

Walkway

Hanger cables link the roadway deck to the cable bands above.

Workers bolt on a roadway section.

Winches lift a roadway section into position.

Believe it or not!
After carefully cleaning the steel deck, workers apply a layer of heavy-duty Bostik glue to stick the asphalt road surface to the deck.

Aircraft warning light

Cable saddle

Elevator

Mind the gap
At each tower, roller joints separate overlapping sections of roadway. Without these joints, a large gap would open up in cold weather as the steel deck contracts.

Roller joint

Welding deck

The cable is coated with red lead and bound with galvanized wire.

Painting the cable

"Wheee!"

Workers add layers of bitumen paint to protect the bridge deck.

Crash barrier cable

The last lift
When the final section was hoisted into place in 1980, the Humber Bridge became the world's then-longest single-span suspension bridge.

Finishing off

1. The steel cables that supported the temporary walkways are used to make crash barriers for the finished roadway, which is now paved.

2. Five coats of weather-resistant paint protect the bridge's steel structure from the damp sea air.

3. Painters use a hanging platform to reach the underside of the bridge.

4. As the painters finish their work, electricians wire up the roadway lights and signs, ready for the grand opening.

Rolling chippings into hot asphalt

Road surface

Laying Bostik

Connecting the electric power

Painting the cables

"I get to drive the first truck across!"

A pontoon nears its final position.

Road deck

Tug boats and gigantic outboard motors maneuver the pontoons into the correct position.

Spray painting from a hanging platform

1. Distant factories make and paint 3,000 stiffened steel plates and ship them to the bridge site for assembly.

2. On the river banks near the bridge, welders construct the roadway as 124 boxes. These sections, each as big as a two-story house, journey by rail and barge before winches lift them into position.

3. A stillage (huge steel framework) holds the panels in position while welders join them and painters spray the welds with protective zinc.

4. A huge gantry crane lifts completed roadway sections onto the pontoons (barges) which float them underneath the completed cables.

5. Winches lift the roadway sections more than 100 ft (30 m) for bolting to the hangers.

Welding box section

A crane lifts the steel plate sections into the stillage.

Spraying with zinc

Close-up of gantry wheels

Close-up of winch

Box section joints are sprayed with zinc.

"We are going to help push the pontoon!"

Pontoons transport the roadway sections to the bridge.

A huge gantry crane stacks the steel roadway sections until they are needed at the construction site.

The assembled box sections are stored on bogies (sets of four wheels) running on two railway tracks.

Workers assemble the steel plate sections that will make up the roadway boxes.

Stillage

Close-up of welding

First stage

The gigantic first stage was the height of a 10-story building, and when filled with propellant, it made up half the weight of the rocket. Six moving vans would fit easily inside its cavernous tanks. These tanks fed fuel and oxidizer to five F1 rocket engines. The most powerful rocket engines ever built, they lifted the vast launcher to a height of 38 miles (61 km) in just 2.5 minutes.

1. The first stage separated after 30 seconds, when explosives blasted off the interstage ring. Although it was the height of a house and traveling at 6,000 mph (10,000 kph), the ring had to slip past the second-stage engines without touching them.

2. In an old room heater, paraffin burns with a cosy glow. The motors of the first stage use this same fuel. When mixed with pure oxygen, paraffin explodes, producing enough power to lift the 3,048-ton (2,766-tonne) launch vehicle high into the air. The intensity of the heat given off would be enough to set fire to a carpet 2 miles (3 km) away.

The Vehicle Assembly Building

The gigantic launch vehicle makes NASA workers look like ants by comparison. They put together the rocket inside a specially built hangar called a Vehicle Assembly Building. It was the largest building in the world on its completion, and it is big enough to enclose 3,700 family homes.

The power of the F1 engines pressed the astronauts into their seats with a force of 4.5 g (4.5 times normal gravity). Astronauts describe this as an "eyeballs-in" g-force.

Fuel

Liquid oxygen

Fuel

Chester refused to light the rocket motors with a match, so instead, engineers pumped hypergol into the engine. When this liquid comes into contact with air, it bursts into flame, igniting the paraffin/oxygen mixture.

The engines were bolted to thrust posts on the enormous, strong thrust structure, which carried the whole weight of the fueled launcher.

Fin

Small rockets, called ullage rockets, provided artificial gravity to ensure that the fuel and oxidizer covered the outlets when the engines fired.

TV cameras linked to fiber optics

Weightlessness and fuel

In near-zero gravity conditions, liquid fuel and oxidizer float freely inside the tanks. This means that vapor, not liquid, could flow to the engines, stopping them from burning. Firing small "ullage" rockets prevented this from happening. By accelerating Saturn V for just a moment, the ullage rockets pushed the fuel and oxidizer to the bottom of the tanks, where the outlets were. The main engines could then fire safely.

The "Range Safety System" consisted of explosive charges designed to blow up the launcher if it strayed from course, thereby protecting the range (launch site) and anyone in the path of the runaway rocket.

Despite the huge size of the launcher, it was not heavy until the fuel tanks were full. Ocean-going ships transported the launcher to a dock near the launch site in Florida. Some smaller sections even traveled in a specially modified aircraft.

The walls of each fuel tank had eight layers.

Fiber optics relay images from lenses monitoring the engines to TV cameras placed a safe distance from the flames.

Electrical equipment and batteries provided power for controlling the first stage and for measuring its performance. For greater reliability, there were two complete sets; if one failed, the other took over automatically.

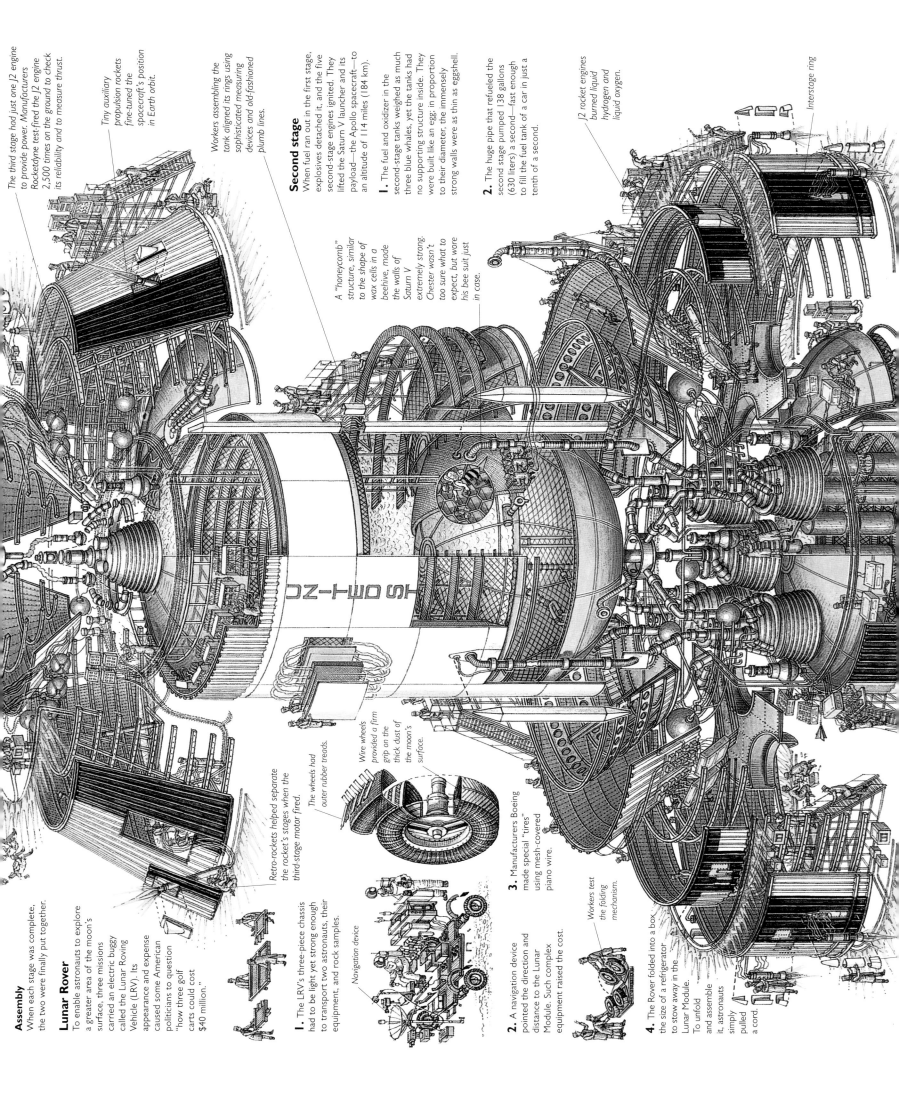

Second stage

When fuel ran out in the first stage, explosives detached it, and the five second-stage engines ignited. They lifted the Saturn V launcher and its payload—the Apollo spacecraft—to an altitude of 114 miles (184 km).

The third stage had just one J2 engine to provide power. Manufacturers Rocketdyne test-fired the J2 engine 2,500 times on the ground to check its reliability and to measure thrust.

Tiny auxiliary propulsion rockets fine-tuned the spacecraft's position in Earth orbit.

Workers assembling the tank aligned its rings using sophisticated measuring devices and old-fashioned plumb lines.

1. The fuel and oxidizer in the second-stage tanks weighed as much as three blue whales, yet the tanks had no supporting structure inside. They were built like an egg: in proportion to their diameter, the immensely strong walls were as thin as an eggshell.

2. The huge pipe that refueled the second stage pumped 138 gallons (630 liters) a second—fast enough to fill the fuel tank of a car in just a tenth of a second.

J2 rocket engines burned liquid hydrogen and liquid oxygen.

Interstage ring

A "honeycomb" structure, similar to the shape of wax cells in a beehive, made the walls of Saturn V extremely strong. Chester wasn't too sure what to expect, but wore his bee suit just in case.

Assembly

When each stage was complete, the two were finally put together.

Lunar Rover

To enable astronauts to explore a greater area of the moon's surface, three missions carried an electric buggy called the Lunar Roving Vehicle (LRV). Its appearance and expense caused some American politicians to question "how three golf carts could cost $40 million."

1. The LRV's three-piece chassis had to be light yet strong enough to transport two astronauts, their equipment, and rock samples.

Navigation device

2. A navigation device pointed the direction and distance to the Lunar Module. Such complex equipment raised the cost.

Retro-rockets helped separate the rocket's stages when the third-stage motor fired.

The wheels had outer rubber treads.

Wire wheels provided a firm grip on the thick dust of the moon's surface.

3. Manufacturers Boeing made special "tires" using mesh-covered piano wire.

Workers test the folding mechanism.

4. The Rover folded into a box the size of a refrigerator to stow away in the Lunar Module. To unfold and assemble it, astronauts simply pulled a cord.

Car

Most modern car factories use robots for routine tasks such as welding and painting. Humans keep production flowing smoothly and monitor quality.

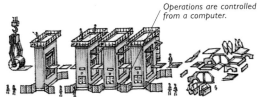

Operations are controlled from a computer.

"All work and no play makes Jack a very dull robot!"

Robot

Laser beams measure the body to check welding accuracy.

The painting process now begins.

1. Steel arrives on rolls. Gigantic presses squeeze the flat sheets into shape.

2. The car emerges from the press shop in the form of more than 60 individual panels.

3. Robots assemble the panels. They weld more accurately than humans and don't get sick.

4. Workers fit the doors, trunk, and hood, then sand smooth the bare metal body.

Brake test

Sealant spray and wax

Wash and dry

Testing the engine

Fitting doors

Marriage conveyor

Making seats

Making dashboards

16. Now the doors go back on, and the car gets a test and wash. The final steps are a sealant spray, a wax, and a brake test.

15. At this point, a specialist adds an annoying, elusive rattle and installs the famous "new car" smell.

14. The "marriage conveyor" brings together the body and the engine components.

Coin

Making coins is an ancient craft. It could be dangerous—in the 16th century, coin makers at London's Mint (coin factory) were made sick by fumes from the melting metal. Coins have been mass-produced since the 18th century, but the tools for making them have changed over time.

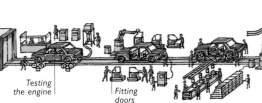

"What a relief!"

Electrotype, a copy in metal

Old-fashioned reducing machine

Steel master punch

Plaster relief

Copper ingot

Nickel is supplied in the form of pellets.

1. Copper is the main raw material for coins, although zinc and tin can also be used. Nickel is added to make the coins harder.

2. A coin starts life in a designer's studio. Then an artist uses plaster to make a relief model many times bigger than the final coin.

3. Today, the plaster model is scanned and sent digitally to a cutting machine, which cuts a replica at a much smaller size onto a steel master punch.

4. Until the late 1990s, however, the master punch would be created like this: workers first made a large metal copy of the plaster model. This was placed in a mechanical reducing machine that cut an exact but smaller replica onto a steel master punch.

6. The rolling mill rolls ingots of cupronickel alloy into thin strips up to ⅔ mile (1 km) long.

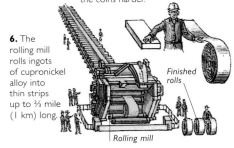

Finished rolls

Rolling mill

7. A blanking machine stamps out the basic round coin shape from the roll of alloy.

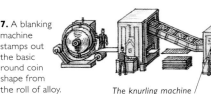

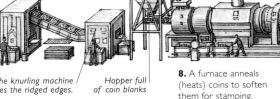

Polishing

The knurling machine makes the ridged edges.

Hopper full of coin blanks

8. A furnace anneals (heats) coins to soften them for stamping.

9. After processing, the coin blanks are dull. A polish brightens them up again.

Armor

Well-made armor fit like a good suit, and even fat knights could easily mount a horse. The invention of guns made armor obsolete; making the metal thick enough to stop bullets made armor too heavy to wear.

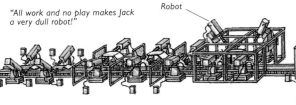

Clients chose their armor from a pattern book.

Marking metal

Shears were anchored in a tree trunk.

Bellows blasted air through the fuel in the furnace to make it burn more fiercely.

The armorer toughened the plates by packing them in red-hot charcoal. Carbon mixed with the iron, turning it to harder steel.

1. Good-quality armor was made to measure. Mail-order clients sent the armorer wax models of their limbs.

2. The armorer marked metal sheets with the outline of the different parts of the suit.

3. Next, the armorer or an apprentice cut out the basic shapes with large shears.

Apprentices moved the plates from the forge to the workshop.

Heating plates

The plates were shaped on a small anvil.

Hot plates were dunked in water to temper them.

Polishing wheel

"Let me out of here!"

4. By carefully filing the edges of each plate, workers made sure that the suit fit exactly.

5. Polishing was slow. To speed the process, armorers used large polishing wheels.

6. Decorating armor made it more expensive. The best suits were etched with elaborate patterns.

"I hope it's strong enough!"

Making a suit of armor took about 6 weeks.

7. A locksmith made and attached the detailed pieces, such as the hinges, buckles, and clasps.

8. Armorers tested their product by firing a crossbow at it. The dent this left demonstrated the armor's strength.

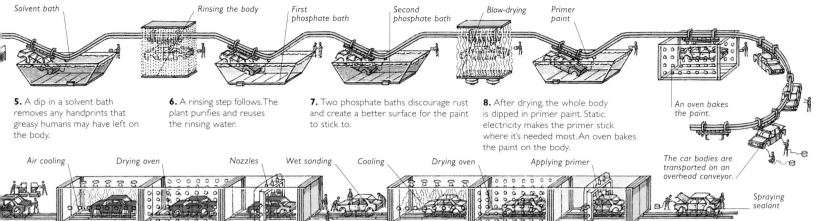

Solvent bath | *Rinsing the body* | *First phosphate bath* | *Second phosphate bath* | *Blow-drying* | *Primer paint*

An oven bakes the paint.

5. A dip in a solvent bath removes any handprints that greasy humans may have left on the body.

6. A rinsing step follows. The plant purifies and reuses the rinsing water.

7. Two phosphate baths discourage rust and create a better surface for the paint to stick to.

8. After drying, the whole body is dipped in primer paint. Static electricity makes the primer stick where it's needed most. An oven bakes the paint on the body.

The car bodies are transported on an overhead conveyor.

Air cooling | *Drying oven* | *Nozzles* | *Wet sanding* | *Cooling* | *Drying oven* | *Applying primer*

Spraying sealant

13. The car is polished, and workers take off the doors so the dashboard and seats can be installed.

12. Spinning bell-shaped nozzles spray on the colored paint layer, and an oven bakes the paint hard. Then jets of air cool the body.

11. Workers wet sand the body to provide a firm surface for the next coat of paint.

10. Another coat of primer paint is applied. From this point on, all operations take place in filtered air, because specks of dust would spoil the car's shiny finish.

9. Next, workers spray sealant over areas of the car that might rust easily.

The master punch stamps a matrix. | *The matrix stamps a working punch.* | *The working punch stamps the design onto a die.* | *"Too dull."* | *"That's better!"*

Matrix | *Finished die*

5. The master punch is used to make a matrix (negative impression) and the matrix to make a working punch. From this punch, workers make a die, which is fitted into the coining press.

Put on your sunglasses!
Machines measure precisely the shininess of coins, and the mint polishes them to the level of brightness each government demands.

Stamping | *Press stamps coin.* | *Finished coin*

10. The faces of the coin are stamped by the press. Then they are checked, weighed, and packed.

Worth their money?
Coins are expensive to make, and the cost of making one is far higher than its value.

Plastic bottle

Plastic bottles are made by a process called injection blow molding.

Molten plastic

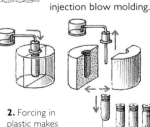

1. The blank mold closes around a tube that will fill it with molten plastic.

2. Forcing in plastic makes a parison, or bottle blank.

Compressed air expands the molten parison into a bottle.

Air tank | *Blanks are released* | *Bottle necks*

3. The blank is moved to a larger, bottle-shaped mold, ready for heating and blowing.

The finished bottles are ready for filling.

Water cools mold

4. Forcing air into the heated blank inflates it to fill the mold.

5. After cooling, the mold opens and the bottle drops out.

Drinking water

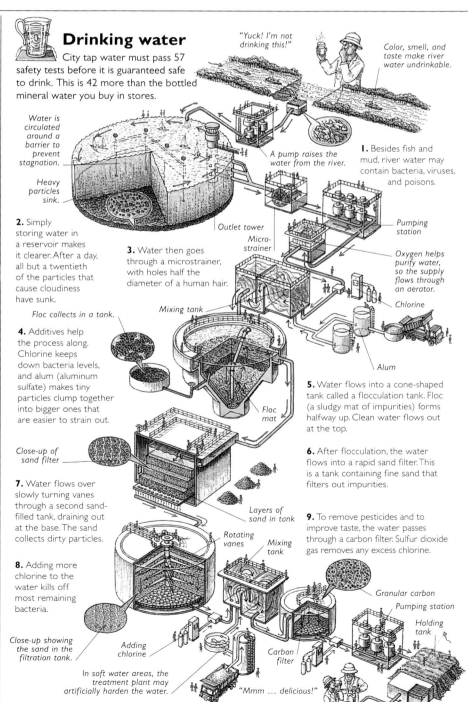

City tap water must pass 57 safety tests before it is guaranteed safe to drink. This is 42 more than the bottled mineral water you buy in stores.

"Yuck! I'm not drinking this!"

Color, smell, and taste make river water undrinkable.

Water is circulated around a barrier to prevent stagnation.

Heavy particles sink.

A pump raises the water from the river.

1. Besides fish and mud, river water may contain bacteria, viruses, and poisons.

Outlet tower

Microstrainer

Pumping station

Oxygen helps purify water, so the supply flows through an aerator.

Chlorine

2. Simply storing water in a reservoir makes it clearer. After a day, all but a twentieth of the particles that cause cloudiness have sunk.

3. Water then goes through a microstrainer, with holes half the diameter of a human hair.

Floc collects in a tank.

Mixing tank

Alum

4. Additives help the process along. Chlorine keeps down bacteria levels, and alum (aluminum sulfate) makes tiny particles clump together into bigger ones that are easier to strain out.

Floc mat

5. Water flows into a cone-shaped tank called a flocculation tank. Floc (a sludgy mat of impurities) forms halfway up. Clean water flows out at the top.

Close-up of sand filter

6. After flocculation, the water flows into a rapid sand filter. This is a tank containing fine sand that filters out impurities.

7. Water flows over slowly turning vanes through a second sand-filled tank, draining out at the base. The sand collects dirty particles.

Layers of sand in tank

Rotating vanes | *Mixing tank*

9. To remove pesticides and to improve taste, the water passes through a carbon filter. Sulfur dioxide gas removes any excess chlorine.

8. Adding more chlorine to the water kills off most remaining bacteria.

Granular carbon

Pumping station

Holding tank

Close-up showing the sand in the filtration tank.

Adding chlorine

Carbon filter

In soft water areas, the treatment plant may artificially harden the water.

"Mmm ... delicious!"

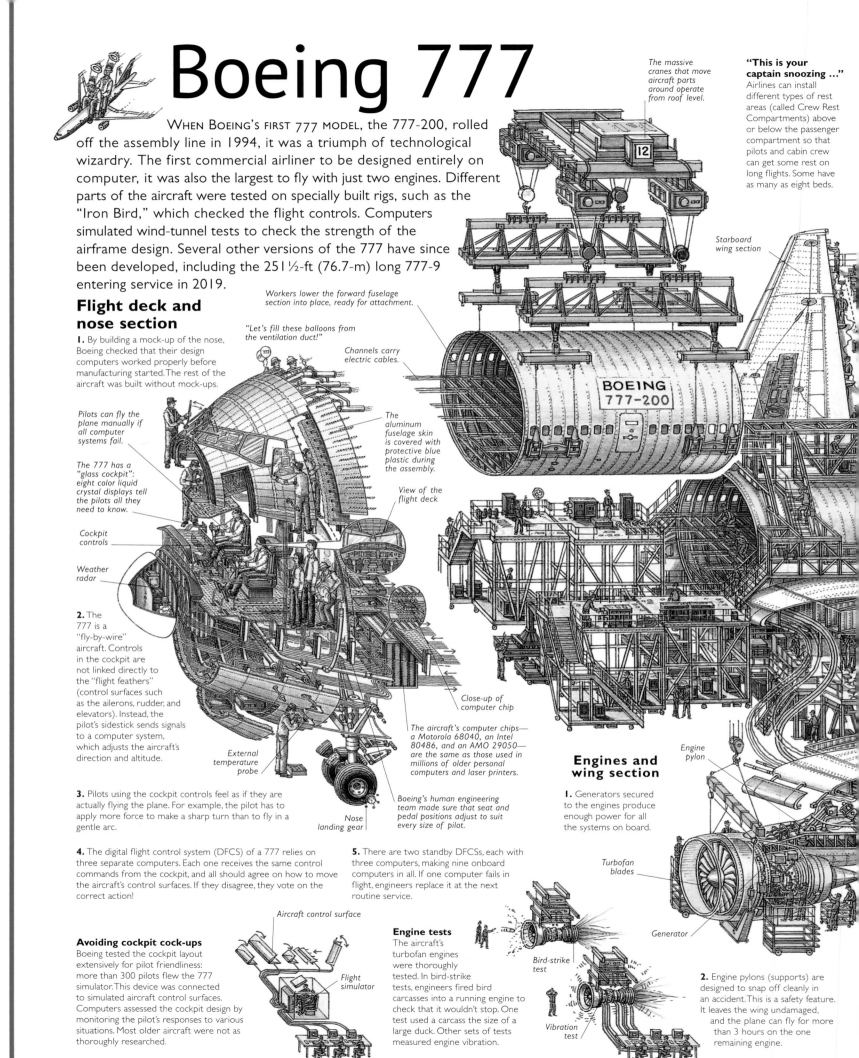

Boeing 777

WHEN BOEING'S FIRST 777 MODEL, the 777-200, rolled off the assembly line in 1994, it was a triumph of technological wizardry. The first commercial airliner to be designed entirely on computer, it was also the largest to fly with just two engines. Different parts of the aircraft were tested on specially built rigs, such as the "Iron Bird," which checked the flight controls. Computers simulated wind-tunnel tests to check the strength of the airframe design. Several other versions of the 777 have since been developed, including the 251½-ft (76.7-m) long 777-9 entering service in 2019.

The massive cranes that move aircraft parts around operate from roof level.

"This is your captain snoozing ..." Airlines can install different types of rest areas (called Crew Rest Compartments) above or below the passenger compartment so that pilots and cabin crew can get some rest on long flights. Some have as many as eight beds.

Starboard wing section

Flight deck and nose section

1. By building a mock-up of the nose, Boeing checked that their design computers worked properly before manufacturing started. The rest of the aircraft was built without mock-ups.

Workers lower the forward fuselage section into place, ready for attachment.

"Let's fill these balloons from the ventilation duct!"

Channels carry electric cables.

Pilots can fly the plane manually if all computer systems fail.

The 777 has a "glass cockpit": eight color liquid crystal displays tell the pilots all they need to know.

The aluminum fuselage skin is covered with protective blue plastic during the assembly.

View of the flight deck

Cockpit controls

Weather radar

2. The 777 is a "fly-by-wire" aircraft. Controls in the cockpit are not linked directly to the "flight feathers" (control surfaces such as the ailerons, rudder, and elevators). Instead, the pilot's sidestick sends signals to a computer system, which adjusts the aircraft's direction and altitude.

Close-up of computer chip

The aircraft's computer chips— a Motorola 68040, an Intel 80486, and an AMO 29050— are the same as those used in millions of older personal computers and laser printers.

External temperature probe

3. Pilots using the cockpit controls feel as if they are actually flying the plane. For example, the pilot has to apply more force to make a sharp turn than to fly in a gentle arc.

Nose landing gear

Boeing's human engineering team made sure that seat and pedal positions adjust to suit every size of pilot.

Engines and wing section

1. Generators secured to the engines produce enough power for all the systems on board.

Engine pylon

4. The digital flight control system (DFCS) of a 777 relies on three separate computers. Each one receives the same control commands from the cockpit, and all should agree on how to move the aircraft's control surfaces. If they disagree, they vote on the correct action!

5. There are two standby DFCSs, each with three computers, making nine onboard computers in all. If one computer fails in flight, engineers replace it at the next routine service.

Turbofan blades

Generator

Avoiding cockpit cock-ups

Boeing tested the cockpit layout extensively for pilot friendliness: more than 300 pilots flew the 777 simulator. This device was connected to simulated aircraft control surfaces. Computers assessed the cockpit design by monitoring the pilot's responses to various situations. Most older aircraft were not as thoroughly researched.

Aircraft control surface

Flight simulator

Engine tests

The aircraft's turbofan engines were thoroughly tested. In bird-strike tests, engineers fired bird carcasses into a running engine to check that it wouldn't stop. One test used a carcass the size of a large duck. Other sets of tests measured engine vibration.

Bird-strike test

Vibration test

2. Engine pylons (supports) are designed to snap off cleanly in an accident. This is a safety feature. It leaves the wing undamaged, and the plane can fly for more than 3 hours on the one remaining engine.

Fuselage and passenger compartment

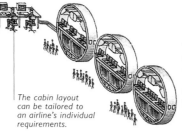

1. Once the fuselage sections are joined, workers install heating, air conditioning, and electrical equipment. Special seat rails allow the seating arrangement to be changed easily: it takes just 4 hours to replace seats with an extra lavatory (compared to 2 days on a 747).

2. Temperatures at cruising altitude are as low as -67°F (-55°C), so workers pack fireproof insulation panels between the inner and outer layers of the plane's fuselage.

The cabin layout can be tailored to an airline's individual requirements.

Pack them in!
The circular shape of the cabin allows airlines to pack in economy class seats 10 abreast. Business class passengers sit eight abreast, and first class passengers sit six abreast.

3. As the passenger cabin takes shape, workers install the in-flight entertainment system. At the time, the entertainment system alone was as complex as a whole aircraft had been 5 years earlier.

4. The overhead luggage lockers are easy to install and remove. Airlines can move the lockers around without disturbing the ducting above.

5. Moisture condensing on the aircraft's cold skin gives designers headaches, because it causes corrosion, and can drip onto passengers' heads. Boeing solved the problem simply by tying sponges to the roof struts.

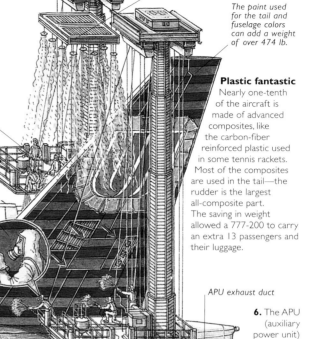

Huge overhead heaters dry the paintwork on the aircraft.

The paint used for the tail and fuselage colors can add a weight of over 474 lb.

Ventilation ducts

Roof strut

Fireproof insulation blanket

Workers painting the huge tailfin work from platforms.

Workers spray paint the tail section.

Worker installs emergency exit door.

Honeycomb floor panel

Cockpit voice recorder (records the voices of the flight crew)

Plastic fantastic
Nearly one-tenth of the aircraft is made of advanced composites, like the carbon-fiber reinforced plastic used in some tennis rackets. Most of the composites are used in the tail—the rudder is the largest all-composite part. The saving in weight allowed a 777-200 to carry an extra 13 passengers and their luggage.

APU exhaust duct

6. The APU (auxiliary power unit) at the rear of the aircraft powers electrical systems when the main engines are turned off.

Passenger compartment rear pressure bulkhead (wall)

Close-up of riveting

Installing window

Port elevator

Port tailplane

Brown paper masks the unpainted areas.

On sections of the aircraft nearer to the ground, workers use an elevating platform.

7. The designers of the 777 paid special attention to the lavatories. Slam-proof seats make the journey more peaceful for passengers sitting nearby.

8. "Liquid leakage" from the lavatories was a serious source of corrosion on earlier aircraft. Because the lavatories can be repositioned easily on a 777, the designers incorporated flooring containing special alloy metals to compensate for passengers with poor aim.

Checked luggage hold

Port spoiler

Port wing fuel tank

Port aileron

9. The spray painting team coat the exterior of the aircraft with paint to a depth of exactly 75 thousandths of a millimeter. A thinner layer would not provide enough protection; too much paint adds to the aircraft's weight and fuel bill.

10. The 777-200 burns one-third less fuel than a 747 but still requires four road tankers to fill its tanks. Passengers could get to their destination using half as much fuel if—instead of flying in a 777—they drove there by car.

Folded wingtip

The folding wingtip section was designed on computer.

But do they flap?
The plane's wings were also designed on computer. They were subjected to extensive simulator testing before designers joined them to the fuselage.

Wind tunnel test

3. On the 777-200's huge wings, there is enough space to park 42 cars.

4. The outer 21 ft 4 in (6.5 m) of each wing can fold up so that the 777-200 can use airport bays designed for much smaller aircraft.

5. Computer-controlled machines secure the rivets that hold many parts of the aircraft together. In 10 seconds, the machine drills, reams, and countersinks the hole; inserts and tightens the rivet; and shaves and smooths down the rivet head. The wings alone have 68,000 rivets and bolts.

Riveting machine

Engineers design the wings on computers.

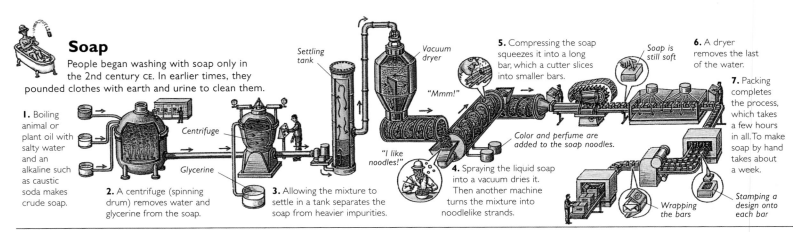

Soap

People began washing with soap only in the 2nd century CE. In earlier times, they pounded clothes with earth and urine to clean them.

1. Boiling animal or plant oil with salty water and an alkaline such as caustic soda makes crude soap.

2. A centrifuge (spinning drum) removes water and glycerine from the soap.

3. Allowing the mixture to settle in a tank separates the soap from heavier impurities.

4. Spraying the liquid soap into a vacuum dries it. Then another machine turns the mixture into noodlelike strands.

5. Compressing the soap squeezes it into a long bar, which a cutter slices into smaller bars.

6. A dryer removes the last of the water.

7. Packing completes the process, which takes a few hours in all. To make soap by hand takes about a week.

Settling tank

Vacuum dryer

Centrifuge

Glycerine

"Mmm!"

"I like noodles!"

Soap is still soft

Color and perfume are added to the soap noodles.

Wrapping the bars

Stamping a design onto each bar

Aluminum foil

The metal foil we now use to cover leftovers was once as valuable as silver and used only for jewelry and trinkets.

1. Furnaces melt raw aluminum metal, and foundry workers pour it into molds to make large ingots. After cutting them into smaller pieces, furnaces heat the ingots to soften them.

2. The hot ingot is placed on a conveyor belt, which moves it back and forth between heavy rollers. Workers move the rollers closer together on each pass to create a long slab.

3. Once the slab has cooled, more rollers flatten it into a roll of thin foil. Annealing (heating in a furnace) makes the foil flexible and sterilizes it.

By the last rolling, the ingots have turned into foil.

4. Machines wind the foil onto cardboard tubes, and workers pack them into boxes. Other machines shape thicker foil into food containers.

Cutting ingots

Casting ingots

The hot slab is ready for rolling.

Roller

The ingot moves back and forth between the rollers.

The ingot has now cooled, ready for further rolling.

Cardboard tubes

Roll of foil

Filling boxes

Finished roll

"Rats! Foiled again!"

Light load

Aluminum became more widely available after 1854, when French Emperor Napoleon III (1808–1873) thought of using it to make lightweight equipment for his army.

Nuclear power

Splitting an atom releases vast amounts of energy. Just two tiny pellets of uranium fuel can generate one person's annual electricity supply.

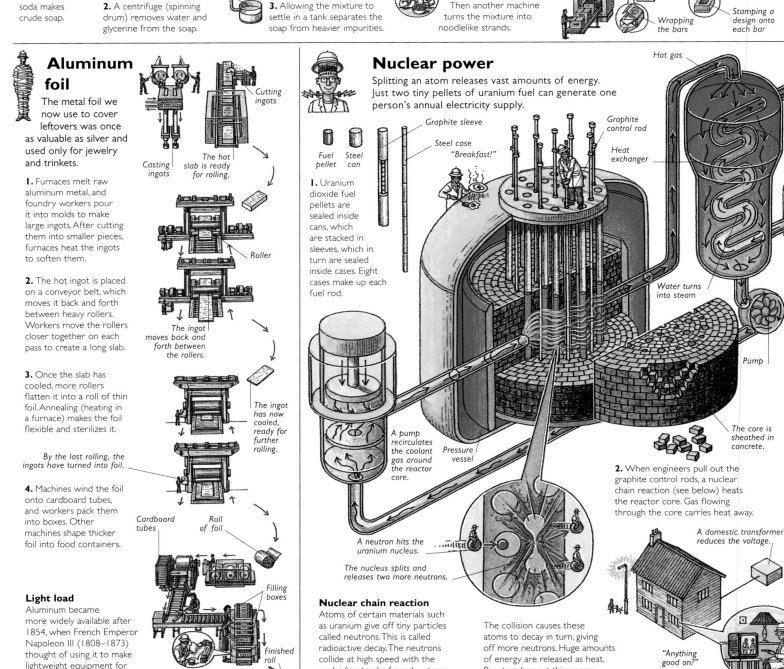

1. Uranium dioxide fuel pellets are sealed inside cans, which are stacked in sleeves, which in turn are sealed inside cases. Eight cases make up each fuel rod.

Fuel pellet

Steel can

Graphite sleeve

Steel case "Breakfast!"

Graphite control rod

Heat exchanger

Hot gas

Water turns into steam

Pump

The core is sheathed in concrete.

A pump recirculates the coolant gas around the reactor core.

Pressure vessel

2. When engineers pull out the graphite control rods, a nuclear chain reaction (see below) heats the reactor core. Gas flowing through the core carries heat away.

A neutron hits the uranium nucleus.

The nucleus splits and releases two more neutrons.

A domestic transformer reduces the voltage.

"Anything good on?"

Nuclear chain reaction

Atoms of certain materials such as uranium give off tiny particles called neutrons. This is called radioactive decay. The neutrons collide at high speed with the nuclei (centers) of nearby atoms.

The collision causes these atoms to decay in turn, giving off more neutrons. Huge amounts of energy are released as heat. Reactors harvest this energy.

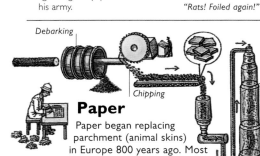

Debarking

Chipping

Paper

Paper began replacing parchment (animal skins) in Europe 800 years ago. Most paper today is made from wood pulp.

1. The logs arrive at the factory, and a machine cuts them up into chips. The chips then pass through a digester, which reduces them to stock (fibers and water).

2. The stock spreads from a slot onto a wire belt, draining off excess water.

3. Then the paper begins a long drying process. It passes between heated drums, which drive off most of the surplus water as steam.

Digester uses steam and heat

Washer

Bleacher

Stock tank

The stock moves onto a wire belt.

Rollers draw paper over felt blankets.

Heated drum

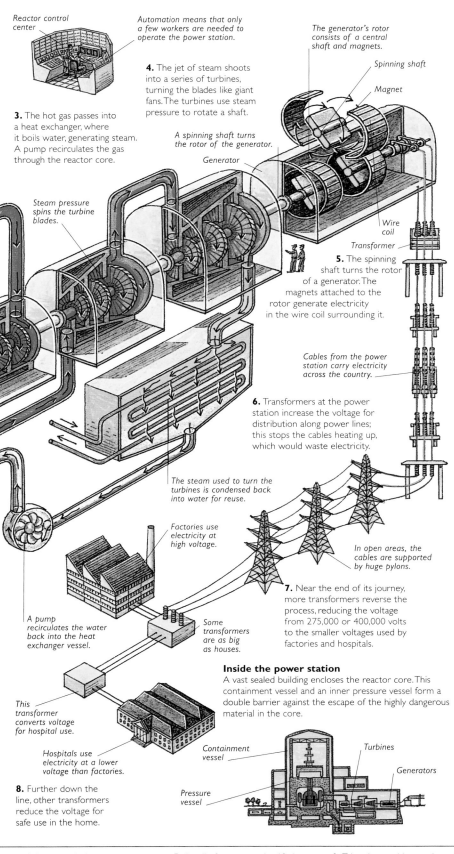

Reactor control center

Automation means that only a few workers are needed to operate the power station.

The generator's rotor consists of a central shaft and magnets.

Spinning shaft

Magnet

4. The jet of steam shoots into a series of turbines, turning the blades like giant fans. The turbines use steam pressure to rotate a shaft.

3. The hot gas passes into a heat exchanger, where it boils water, generating steam. A pump recirculates the gas through the reactor core.

A spinning shaft turns the rotor of the generator.

Generator

Steam pressure spins the turbine blades.

Wire coil

Transformer

5. The spinning shaft turns the rotor of a generator. The magnets attached to the rotor generate electricity in the wire coil surrounding it.

Cables from the power station carry electricity across the country.

6. Transformers at the power station increase the voltage for distribution along power lines; this stops the cables heating up, which would waste electricity.

The steam used to turn the turbines is condensed back into water for reuse.

Factories use electricity at high voltage.

In open areas, the cables are supported by huge pylons.

7. Near the end of its journey, more transformers reverse the process, reducing the voltage from 275,000 or 400,000 volts to the smaller voltages used by factories and hospitals.

A pump recirculates the water back into the heat exchanger vessel.

Some transformers are as big as houses.

This transformer converts voltage for hospital use.

Hospitals use electricity at a lower voltage than factories.

8. Further down the line, other transformers reduce the voltage for safe use in the home.

Inside the power station

A vast sealed building encloses the reactor core. This containment vessel and an inner pressure vessel form a double barrier against the escape of the highly dangerous material in the core.

Containment vessel

Turbines

Generators

Pressure vessel

Pipe organ

Playing an 18th-century pipe organ like this one is hard work, as the action is all mechanical. The action of modern instruments is assisted by electricity.

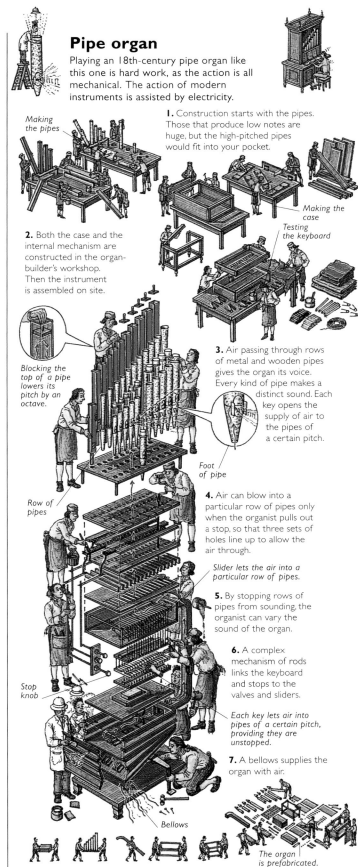

Making the pipes

1. Construction starts with the pipes. Those that produce low notes are huge, but the high-pitched pipes would fit into your pocket.

Making the case

Testing the keyboard

2. Both the case and the internal mechanism are constructed in the organ-builder's workshop. Then the instrument is assembled on site.

Blocking the top of a pipe lowers its pitch by an octave.

3. Air passing through rows of metal and wooden pipes gives the organ its voice. Every kind of pipe makes a distinct sound. Each key opens the supply of air to the pipes of a certain pitch.

Foot of pipe

Row of pipes

4. Air can blow into a particular row of pipes only when the organist pulls out a stop, so that three sets of holes line up to allow the air through.

Slider lets the air into a particular row of pipes.

5. By stopping rows of pipes from sounding, the organist can vary the sound of the organ.

6. A complex mechanism of rods links the keyboard and stops to the valves and sliders.

Stop knob

Each key lets air into pipes of a certain pitch, providing they are unstopped.

7. A bellows supplies the organ with air.

Bellows

The organ is prefabricated.

---

4. Between drying stages, various coating processes improve the surface of the paper. Calendering (pressing between shiny, chilled rollers) polishes and finishes the paper.

Calendering

The finished roll is huge.

5. A roll of paper may be 12 times the width of wallpaper, so workers rewind it and cut the roll to a smaller size.

Rewinding

Cutting

6. Trimming machines reduce the width even further and trim the paper into sheets, ready for packing. Like the other steps, trimming takes place under computer control.

"Phew! That's easier to manage!"

The roll of paper feeds into the trimming machine.

The trimming machine cuts the paper into smaller sheets, ready for packing.

7. After thorough testing for strength, surface qualities, and aerodynamic ability, the paper is packed and dispatched.

"I've always wanted my very own F-18!"

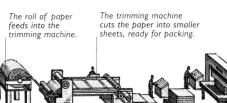

Race car

COMPARING A FORMULA I RACE CAR to a family sedan is like comparing a gown from a top fashion designer to an outfit from a high-street chain store. Every aspect of a race car is made to measure. The driver sits snugly in the cockpit, surrounded by a survival cell made of high-tech materials designed to keep him or her as safe as possible. Design, technology, and rules change from year to year. At the first Formula I race of the season, everyone stares at the new cars, examining every detail and watching how the design affects each car's performance.

The design

Some designers like to start by hand, but today, many use computers even for their initial drawings.

Many teams now use 3D printers to produce accurate models; if not, a modelmaker makes miniature 3D models.

Handmade models are digitized into a 3D computer model by a digitizing arm that traces its contours.

The body of the car

The shape of a car's body has a huge effect on speed, so designers decide this first. Engineers must then find room for all the car's other components—such as the engine and suspension—in the tiny body. To give all cars an equal chance, strict rules govern every construction detail. The model shown here is a classic Ferrari from the mid-1990s.

1. One of the biggest dangers to drivers is a fuel fire. Drivers sit in front of the tank, which at the start of the race contains over 220 lb (100 kg) of highly flammable fuel. Shock-absorbing panels protect the tank, and a puncture-resistant bladder stops fuel leaking in a crash.

2. On a sedan, the suspension smooths the ride, cushioning driver and passengers. On a race car, it must stop the car from bouncing up, as this interrupts the wheels' grip on the track and also reduces the downforce that helps keep the car down on the track at high speeds (very important when taking corners). Its suspension is adjustable within fractions of a millimeter to match different tracks and weather conditions.

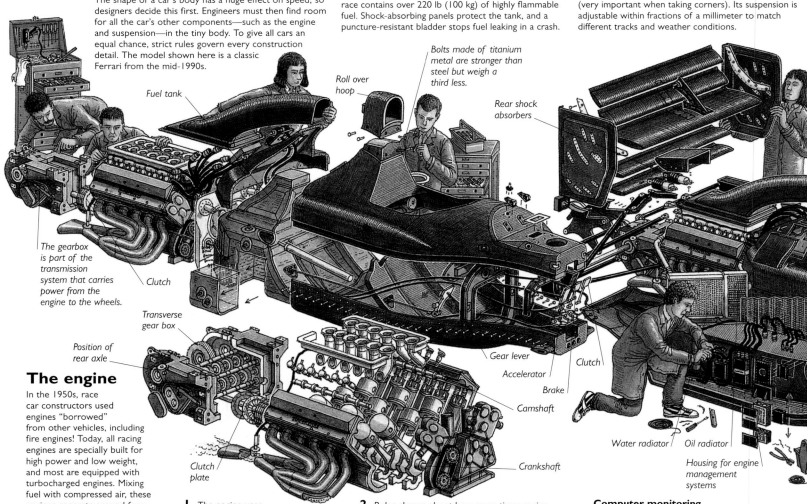

Fuel tank

The gearbox is part of the transmission system that carries power from the engine to the wheels.

Clutch

Transverse gear box

Position of rear axle

Clutch plate

Roll over hoop

Bolts made of titanium metal are stronger than steel but weigh a third less.

Rear shock absorbers

Gear lever

Accelerator

Brake

Clutch

Camshaft

Crankshaft

Water radiator

Oil radiator

Housing for engine management systems

The engine

In the 1950s, race car constructors used engines "borrowed" from other vehicles, including fire engines! Today, all racing engines are specially built for high power and low weight, and most are equipped with turbocharged engines. Mixing fuel with compressed air, these engines generate around four times the power of a typical family car engine.

1. The engine uses less than a third of all the fuel it burns to move the car around the track. More is wasted in noise and heat from the exhaust.

2. Rules change about how many times racing teams can change engines in a season. At one point, mechanics would dismantle the car after each race, remove the engine, and ship it back to the manufacturers. Today, fewer changes are allowed, so the engines must be more reliable.

Computer monitoring

Hundreds of sensors are placed all over the car. They transmit data on all aspects of the car's performance to the team's computer. Each lap of a race can generate up to 35 megabytes of data, which is all analyzed.

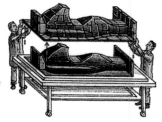

Building the body

A computer-controlled milling machine cuts precise molds for the body from flat panels.

Stacking up the panels and securing them together creates the final form for the mold. These are smoothed by hand.

Fabricators first paint over release agents and wax to prevent sticking, then coat the form with epoxy resin.

Next, the form is carefully covered with multiple layers of carbon fiber sheeting. This is the mold.

To strengthen and harden the body, it is "cured" by being placed in a vacuum bag in an autoclave (pressurized oven).

On computers, engineers plan how the body will fit together with other components. CFD simulations, which mimic the complex airflow around the car, are run repeatedly to improve design. The final digital model guides the cutters of the full-sized molds.

To simulate a race, a huge fan blows air across the model in a wind tunnel and an endless belt turns the wheels. Sensors measure drag, downforce, and vibration. These tests help predict how the car will behave on the track.

While the fan is turned off, engineers run into the tunnel and change tiny details of the car. They have to hurry, because wind tunnel time is very expensive and restricted.

Modifications that improve the flow of air over the model will make the full-sized car go faster.

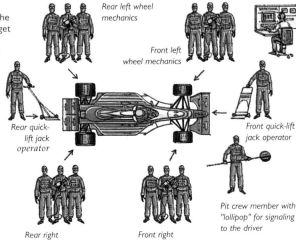

The "clothes" of the car

The flaps, wings, and tires are like the race car's clothes. Engineers decide on the basic outfit at the design stage. But many of these parts are easy to remove. The pit crew exchanges them to make small adjustments to the car's performance. The wings work like an upside-down aircraft wing. The faster the car goes, the more it is pressed to the ground, improving the grip of the tires.

Wings at the front and back create a downward force that is greater than the car's weight.

The finishing touches

Finishing touches include a shiny paint finish and advertising for sponsors—companies that give money to racing teams in exchange for publicity. The more money a sponsor provides, the larger and more prominent their logo appears on the car. The technicians must position the company logos carefully to keep all the sponsors happy.

Six-point harness

The seat is not padded, and the driver feels every bump.

The driver

Drivers wear fireproof clothes made of multiple layers of flame-retardant materials such as Nomex. A special support collar and straps stop the driver's head from hitting the steering wheel or their back from being injured if there is a crash. The eye-slit of the fireproof glass-fiber-reinforced helmet is narrow to protect against flying debris.

Epaulettes are reinforced so the driver can be dragged from a burning wreck.

"Even his underwear is flame resistant!"

Brake pads

The housings for the brakes are designed to channel air across the discs to cool them. As drivers brake, the carbon-fiber discs glow red hot. This car's pads work best at 660–930°F (350–500°C).

The nose is designed to crumple and absorb shock on impact.

The body of the car is made up of multiple layers of light—but tough and strong—carbon fiber. Sandwiched between these layers is a strong, light honeycomb structure.

Racing teams use many different tires, changing them for different circuits and weather conditions.

Front wing

Technicians monitor data on the car's performance.

Pit stop

During a race, cars call in at the pits (small workshops) for new tires and other maintenance. A team of around 20 mechanics and technicians make up the pit crew and work at dizzying speed to get the car back into the race as quickly as possible. With three mechanics on each wheel, changing all four tires takes 3 seconds or less.

"Alright, let's try it again with you in the driver's seat."

Most cars are made from five moldings or less. During assembly, technicians add aluminum bulkheads to strengthen the cockpit.

Before a new car can race, it must pass stringent safety tests and survive simulated side, rear, and front impacts.

Rear left wheel mechanics

Front left wheel mechanics

Rear quick-lift jack operator

Front quick-lift jack operator

Rear right wheel mechanics

Front right wheel mechanics

Pit crew member with "lollipop" for signaling to the driver

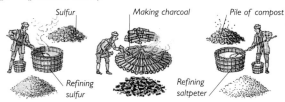

Gunpowder

Old-fashioned explosive gunpowder was made from three elements: 10 parts sulfur, 15 parts charcoal, and 75 parts saltpeter (potassium nitrate).

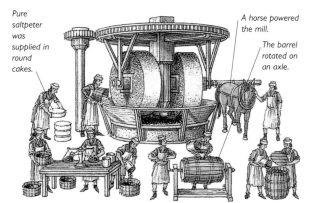

Sulfur
Refining sulfur

Making charcoal

Pile of compost
Refining saltpeter

1. Yellow brimstone (sulfur) was taken from volcanoes. Pure sulfur crackles if you hold it to your ear.

2. Charcoal is made by burning wood without air. A fire was covered with turf to do this.

3. Saltpeter came from nitrogen-rich soils and animal dung. The king's saltpeter men collected it from barns.

Pure saltpeter was supplied in round cakes.

A horse powered the mill.

The barrel rotated on an axle.

4. A huge stone roller, driven by horse or water power, crushed the cakes of purified saltpeter into a fine powder.

5. After weighing out the ingredients, workers tumbled them in a barrel to mix them.

6. The most dangerous step was incorporation. This process mixed the ingredients into grains.

Accidents were common with such a dangerous explosive substance.

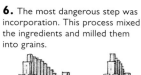

7. Water-powered pestles pounded the mixture once each second. This process took 24 hours.

8. The finished gunpowder grains were now highly explosive. Workers stored them carefully.

Corning

Tumbling

9. Corning (forcing the powder through holes in a parchment sheet) and then tumbling it in a barrel produced larger pellets of explosive.

10. To prevent an explosion, the powder dried in a "gloom stove"—a room heated by the back of a fire burning next door.

Gentle heat dried the powder safely.

Powder sat on racks in the room.

"Stand clear!"

"Fire!"

"Looks good!"

11. Good gunpowder burned cleanly and did not ignite another heap of powder a hand's-width away.

12. Gunpowder was also tested with a cannon, and the penetration of the shot was measured.

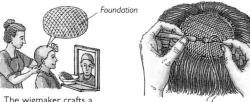

Wig

Wig thieves flourished in crowded 18th-century streets. Sitting on a man's shoulders, a small boy snatched the fashionable wigs from passing heads. Modern wig-wearers face no similar perils!

1. A tailor-made wig needs careful measuring if it is to fit properly and look like real hair.

The foundation rests on a block.

The wig is ready for styling.

Foundation

2. The wigmaker crafts a nylon cap, called a foundation, to hold all the hair in place.

3. The wigmaker knots up to 150,000 hairs individually along a parting.

4. While the wig is being made, it rests on a head-shaped block. The finished wig has long hair.

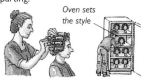

Oven sets the style

5. Back in the salon, the hairdresser cuts and styles the wig as if it was the wearer's real hair.

6. To create curly hair, the hairdresser uses rollers, then sets the style in a cool oven.

7. Elastic and adhesive tape hold the wig in position—even in high winds!

Cathedral

Medieval masons created spectacular cathedrals using simple hand tools. The spire of Strasbourg is the height of a 44-story office building; Amiens Cathedral is so vast that everyone in the city could worship together when it was completed.

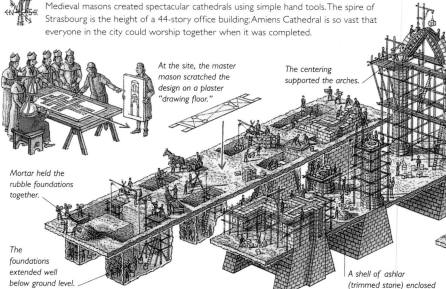

At the site, the master mason scratched the design on a plaster "drawing floor."

The centering supported the arches.

Mortar held the rubble foundations together.

The foundations extended well below ground level.

A shell of ashlar (trimmed stone) enclosed the rubble wall core.

1. The master mason (architect) presented drawings on parchment to show roughly what the building would look like.

2. Workers built the cathedral foundations on solid bedrock, sometimes digging down 33–50 ft (10–15 m).

3. Carpenters built wooden centering as temporary supports for the stone arches. Masons cut stones on the ground to fit.

Brick

Bricks were all handmade until about 1860. Now they are made in factories by machines.

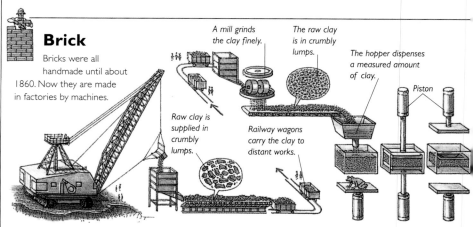

A mill grinds the clay finely.

The raw clay is in crumbly lumps.

The hopper dispenses a measured amount of clay.

Piston

Raw clay is supplied in crumbly lumps.

Railway wagons carry the clay to distant works.

1. A shovel excavator digs out the raw materials (clay or shale) for the bricks.

2. A conveyor belt or train moves the clay from the quarry to the brickworks.

3. Pistons press the semidry clay into a brick-shaped mold, compacting it.

A lead weight

The lead covering the roof of the cathedral was often the most valuable part of the whole building. The amount of metal on a roof could be huge. During the Great Fire of London in 1666, the roof of Old St. Paul's Cathedral melted and sent a river of molten lead flowing through the streets.

Masons used ladders and scaffolding to reach their work.

"Hmm, this looks like it will hold for a few centuries!"

Lead sheeting protected the wooden roof against rain.

Buttresses prevented the walls from splaying out under the weight of the lead roof.

Wooden scaffolding

Slender columns allowed for big windows of colored glass.

Winch lifts stones

Layer of concrete

Vault rib

The mosaic floor maze was for worship: the faithful traced the winding path on their knees.

It's all your vault ...

Vaults were the only way medieval masons could construct a large ceiling area. Only the thick stone ribs needed wooden supports during construction.

1. Masons built the ribs of the vault first.

2. Pieces of wood held up the stones while the mortar between them set.

3. Flat stones were added to create a lightweight ceiling.

4. Finally, a layer of concrete covered the entire vault to seal it.

Building many identical bays extended the cathedral's length.

Athletic shoe

Developing the design for a new athletic shoe takes many years. Only after extensive research and modifications will the shoe go on sale to the public.

"I think it needs a thicker sole."

1. The athletes who will use the shoe are consulted at the design stage.

Trim
Upper
Finished sample shoe
Sole
Cushion
Sole insert

2. A sample shoe is built. Most athletic shoes have five main parts, but there may be many more.

"Pooh! We need to work on the ventilation!"
"It runs by itself!"

3. Field trials are carried out.

Cutting pieces of leather
Sewing machine

4. The shoes are assembled mainly by hand. Workers stitch the uppers and trim, then glue the soles to the uppers.

"Glad we got that ventilation fixed!"

5. The quality of the finished shoes is carefully checked.

4. Masons completed work on one bay (the section between two main columns) before starting the next. Building work stopped in winter, and thatch covered uncompleted walls to prevent damage by rain and frost.

5. Construction of the vaults (arched stone ceilings) was the trickiest part of the entire building job. Carpenters constructed a temporary roof so that masons could then work on the first stage of the vaults protected from the weather.

6. Once the roof was covered with lead, the vaults could be finished and the floor of the cathedral laid. Last of all, the interior was decorated.

7. Building a cathedral took so long that the architect was often dead by the time the cathedral opened. Some cathedrals took hundreds of years to complete.

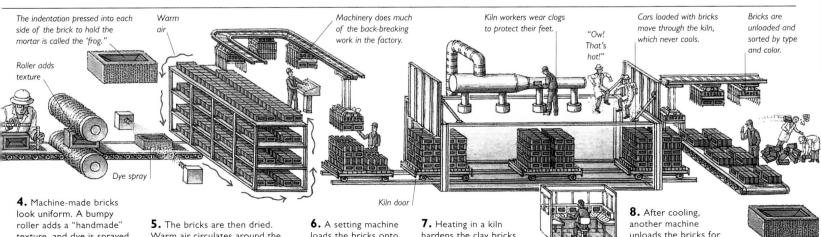

The indentation pressed into each side of the brick to hold the mortar is called the 'frog.'

Roller adds texture

Dye spray

Warm air

Machinery does much of the back-breaking work in the factory.

Kiln workers wear clogs to protect their feet.

"Ow! That's hot!"

Kiln door

Cars loaded with bricks move through the kiln, which never cools.

Bricks are unloaded and sorted by type and color.

4. Machine-made bricks look uniform. A bumpy roller adds a "handmade" texture, and dye is sprayed on to color the brick.

5. The bricks are then dried. Warm air circulates around the bricks, drawing off moisture.

6. A setting machine loads the bricks onto a small car.

7. Heating in a kiln hardens the clay bricks to a stonelike texture.

8. After cooling, another machine unloads the bricks for sorting and packing.

Chocolate bar

Until the early 1900s, chocolate was an occasional treat. But during World War I (1914–1918), bars were packed into soldiers' rucksacks, making it universally popular.

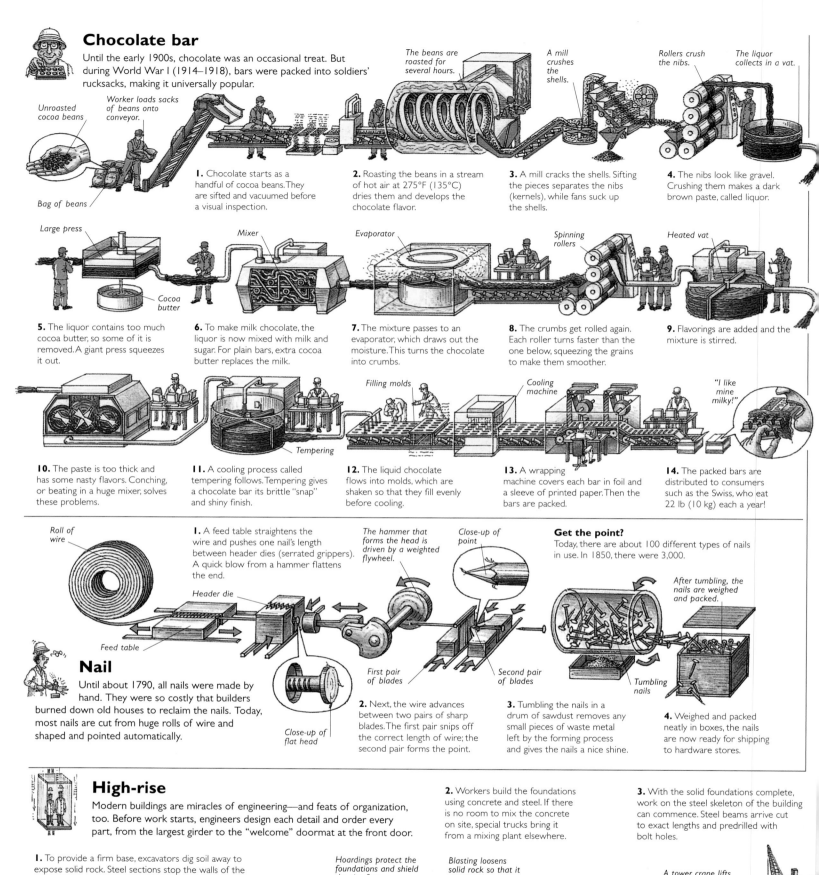

The beans are roasted for several hours.

A mill crushes the shells.

Rollers crush the nibs.

The liquor collects in a vat.

Unroasted cocoa beans

Worker loads sacks of beans onto conveyor.

Bag of beans

1. Chocolate starts as a handful of cocoa beans. They are sifted and vacuumed before a visual inspection.

2. Roasting the beans in a stream of hot air at 275°F (135°C) dries them and develops the chocolate flavor.

3. A mill cracks the shells. Sifting the pieces separates the nibs (kernels), while fans suck up the shells.

4. The nibs look like gravel. Crushing them makes a dark brown paste, called liquor.

Large press

Mixer

Evaporator

Spinning rollers

Heated vat

Cocoa butter

5. The liquor contains too much cocoa butter, so some of it is removed. A giant press squeezes it out.

6. To make milk chocolate, the liquor is now mixed with milk and sugar. For plain bars, extra cocoa butter replaces the milk.

7. The mixture passes to an evaporator, which draws out the moisture. This turns the chocolate into crumbs.

8. The crumbs get rolled again. Each roller turns faster than the one below, squeezing the grains to make them smoother.

9. Flavorings are added and the mixture is stirred.

Filling molds

Cooling machine

"I like mine milky!"

Tempering

10. The paste is too thick and has some nasty flavors. Conching, or beating in a huge mixer, solves these problems.

11. A cooling process called tempering follows. Tempering gives a chocolate bar its brittle "snap" and shiny finish.

12. The liquid chocolate flows into molds, which are shaken so that they fill evenly before cooling.

13. A wrapping machine covers each bar in foil and a sleeve of printed paper. Then the bars are packed.

14. The packed bars are distributed to consumers such as the Swiss, who eat 22 lb (10 kg) each a year!

Roll of wire

1. A feed table straightens the wire and pushes one nail's length between header dies (serrated grippers). A quick blow from a hammer flattens the end.

The hammer that forms the head is driven by a weighted flywheel.

Close-up of point

Get the point?
Today, there are about 100 different types of nails in use. In 1850, there were 3,000.

After tumbling, the nails are weighed and packed.

Header die

Nail

Until about 1790, all nails were made by hand. They were so costly that builders burned down old houses to reclaim the nails. Today, most nails are cut from huge rolls of wire and shaped and pointed automatically.

Feed table

Close-up of flat head

First pair of blades

Second pair of blades

Tumbling nails

2. Next, the wire advances between two pairs of sharp blades. The first pair snips off the correct length of wire; the second pair forms the point.

3. Tumbling the nails in a drum of sawdust removes any small pieces of waste metal left by the forming process and gives the nails a nice shine.

4. Weighed and packed neatly in boxes, the nails are now ready for shipping to hardware stores.

High-rise

Modern buildings are miracles of engineering—and feats of organization, too. Before work starts, engineers design each detail and order every part, from the largest girder to the "welcome" doormat at the front door.

2. Workers build the foundations using concrete and steel. If there is no room to mix the concrete on site, special trucks bring it from a mixing plant elsewhere.

3. With the solid foundations complete, work on the steel skeleton of the building can commence. Steel beams arrive cut to exact lengths and predrilled with bolt holes.

1. To provide a firm base, excavators dig soil away to expose solid rock. Steel sections stop the walls of the excavation from collapsing.

Hoardings protect the foundations and shield the site from onlookers.

Blasting loosens solid rock so that it can be removed.

Cement mixer

A tower crane lifts the steel beams.

Most city center building sites are so small that everything must arrive just at the moment it's needed.

Structural steel for the building travels on a huge truck.

Steel section

Blast mat

Steel beams are unloaded ready for the tower crane to hoist them into place.

False teeth

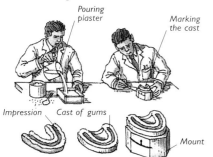

Early dental prostheses (false teeth) were made from gold, iron, or even wood. Today, plastic and porcelain are used to make false teeth that are nearly as good as the real thing.

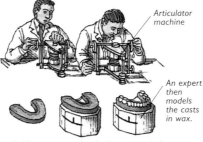

Goo rests in frame

1. Treatment starts with patients biting on dental paste to make an impression of their gums.

Pouring plaster

Marking the cast

Impression   *Cast of gums*

Mount

2. A technician pours plaster into the impression to make casts of the gums, which are then mounted on a base.

Articulator machine

An expert then models the casts in wax.

3. The casts are checked on an articulator machine, which simulates a human jaw. This checks that the two halves fit.

Color matching the teeth

Expert adjusts fit

Teeth are added to test the bite

4. At the dentist's office, the patient tries out the wax model. A technician makes any adjustments needed and fits porcelain teeth.

"Open wide!"

Finished dentures

5. Another casting replaces the wax with plastic. After cleaning the teeth, the dentist gives the patient a bright new smile.

Look out below!

Nausea limits the height of a building. The tallest buildings sway in the wind, making people on the upper floors feel seasick.

The top of the building has a light to warn aircraft.

Decorative copper roof

Air-conditioning equipment

Elevator machinery

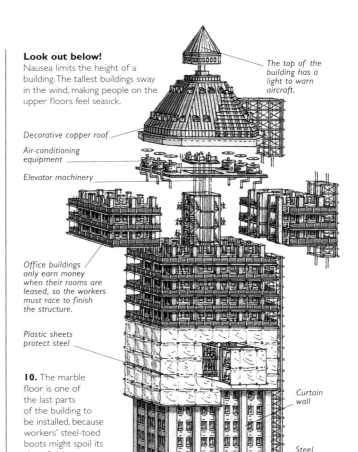

Office buildings only earn money when their rooms are leased, so the workers must race to finish the structure.

Plastic sheets protect steel

Curtain wall

10. The marble floor is one of the last parts of the building to be installed, because workers' steel-toed boots might spoil its clean finish.

Steel frame

9. As the exterior of the building is completed, workers finish the central core. This houses services such as elevators, piping, and staircases. The roof hides the elevator motors and air-conditioning equipment.

An outside elevator is used by the workers until the main interior elevators are finished.

The frame factor

The steel frame is like a skeleton that supports the building. As well as keeping out the weather, the curtain (outside) walls help stop the building from swaying in the wind.

The big cover-up

Each trade covers up the rougher work that went before. Workers apply plasterboard panels to hide wide joints in the concrete; plasterers hide smaller joints between the panels; and painters hide tiny marks in the plaster.

4. As pieces of steel are added, the frame grows taller. Jacks raise the tower crane so that it keeps pace with the height of the frame. Each piece of steel is numbered so that the workers know where it goes.

5. Once the steel frame is complete, workers add rough floors. They pour concrete over a mesh of reinforcing bars or a stiffened deck of steel.

Workers deliberately use curved beams in some parts of the structure. When the beam has weight on it, it straightens out.

Tower crane grows with the structure

Pre-cut piece of steel

Workers install rough floors.

Wall panel

As the building grows, the lower floors are finished, ready for tenants.

6. The scaffolding helps workers reach the exterior. On the upper floors, scaffolding hangs from the building's steel frame.

7. To clad the building, cranes winch the insulated curtain wall panels into position, and workers standing inside the building secure them in place.

8. Once the frame, floors, and walls are in place, contractors can fit the electrical, plumbing, and air-conditioning equipment and install fire sprinklers.

Daily newspaper

When earthquakes strike or wars break out, we want to read all about it as soon as it happens. Many people get their news via the Internet, but printed newspapers are still popular throughout the world. To fill newspapers with eyewitness reports and dramatic pictures, journalists and photographers travel across the globe, often to dangerous places. They send their stories to the newspaper offices, where a team processes the information and decides what is going to be included. The pages are designed and edited on computers, then sent to the printer. Today, newspapers are produced with various levels of computer input, but many are still printed on traditional printing presses, like the one shown here. Although most now send their pages from computer straight to plate, a few still make plates from film in the traditional way.

News gathering

Reporters and photographers travel the country to collect news. Only the larger papers can afford to send journalists abroad to report on international events.

A lot of foreign news comes from news agencies, also known as wire services, that employ journalists and photographers worldwide and sell their articles to different newspapers.

Journalists type their news stories on their phones or laptops and send or "file" them with a newspaper via email, over the Internet, or by satellite phone.

In the newsroom, subeditors, picture editors, and designers lay out each page of the newspaper on computer. Large screens show them how each page will look.

Every day, departmental chiefs of a newspaper meet with the editor to discuss the day's news stories. Together they decide which stories and pictures to include in the following day's newspaper.

News happens 24 hours a day, and the night editor has to be ready to make changes through the night—up until the minute when printing starts in the early hours of the morning.

Some journalists work in the newspaper offices to research and compile facts on background or information articles called features.

Most newspapers keep their selling price down by earning money from advertising. Sales staff sell space in the newspaper, taking down details by phone or email.

Satellite links allow journalists to send in stories from almost anywhere.

When a story arrives at a newspaper, it is routed to the correct desk by computer.

"My truth detector can spot a liar," says Chester.

Platemaking from film

For each page, four separate printing plates are made, one for each color (see below). Technicians first create a copy of the page on clear film in an image-setter. This is passed to a processor that develops the film, creating a negative. In an exposure unit, the film is brought into contact with an aluminum plate coated with a special emulsion. Light shining through the film causes chemical changes in the emulsion. Areas struck by light become greasy so ink will stick to them.

Image setter

Processor

Exposure unit

A machine dries the finished plate

Printing plates are thin enough to wrap around cylinders inside the press.

Printing in color

The paper runs through four units of the press. These are almost identical—the only difference between them is that each prints a different color. The first unit prints the cyan (blue) parts of pictures; the second, the magenta (purple) areas; the third, the yellow areas; and the final unit at the top of the press prints the black areas and the black type. By varying the intensity of these four colors, it is possible to create every color of the rainbow.

Blanket cylinder

Ink roller

Plate cylinder

Dampening rollers

Ink roller

Water spray bar

Ink feed

Ink trough

Ink pump

The third set of rollers prints both sides with the yellow portions of every color picture.

The printing press

When it reaches the printing press, the web runs through the four different color units. A printing plate is secured to one of the rollers in each unit, while other rollers transfer ink from a feed trough. Access points everywhere in the press allow technicians to reach inside for maintenance and adjustment.

The fourth set of rollers prints both sides with the final color of the process—black.

Folding and cutting

After printing, the paper reaches the top of the press. It runs over rollers that direct the web back down again into the folder. The first blade slits the paper in two, then each half passes through a pair of forming rollers that fold it down the middle. Blades cut the paper and the collecting cylinder puts in more folds. The assembled newspaper drops into a paddle-wheel assembly, which then drops the whole thing onto a delivery belt.

Forming rollers

Folding knife and collecting cylinder

Clips secure the newspapers to an endless chain that carries the papers to packing points.

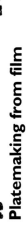

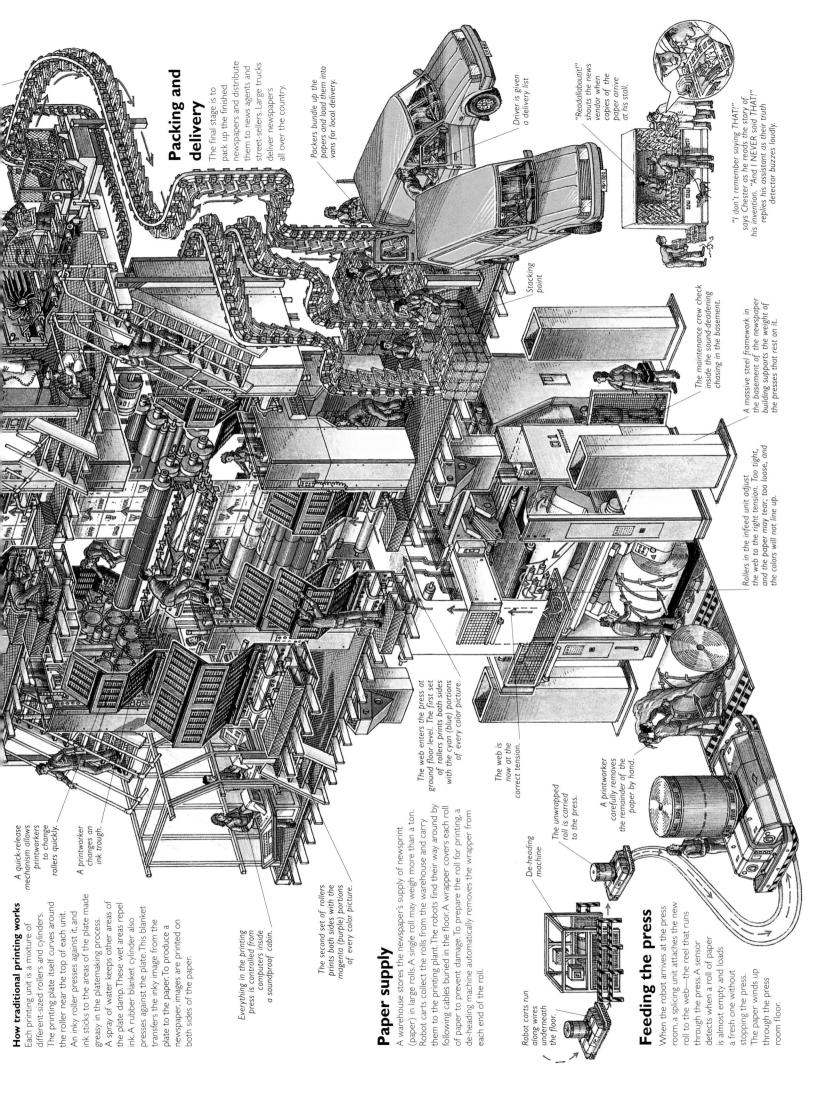

Packing and delivery

The final stage is to pack up the finished newspapers and distribute them to news agents and street-sellers. Large trucks deliver newspapers all over the country.

Packers bundle up the papers and load them into vans for local delivery.

Driver is given a delivery list

"Readallaboutit!" shouts the news vendor when copies of the paper arrive at his stall.

"I don't remember saying THAT!" says Chester as he reads the story of his invention. "And I NEVER said THAT!" replies his assistant as their truth detector buzzes loudly.

Stacking point

The maintenance crew check inside the sound-deadening casing in the basement.

A massive steel framework in the basement of the newspaper building supports the weight of the presses that rest on it.

Rollers in the infeed unit adjust the web to the right tension. Too tight, and the paper may tear; too loose, and the colors will not line up.

How traditional printing works

Each printing unit is a mixture of different-sized rollers and cylinders. The printing plate itself curves around the roller near the top of each unit. An inky roller presses against it, and ink sticks to the areas of the plate made greasy in the platemaking process. A spray of water keeps other areas of the plate damp. These wet areas repel ink. A rubber blanket cylinder also presses against the plate. This blanket transfers the inky image from the plate to the paper. To produce a newspaper, images are printed on both sides of the paper.

A quick-release mechanism allows printworkers to change rollers quickly.

A printworker changes an ink trough.

Everything in the printing press is controlled from computers inside a soundproof cabin.

The second set of rollers prints both sides with the magenta (purple) portions of every color picture.

Paper supply

A warehouse stores the newspaper's supply of newsprint (paper) in large rolls. A single roll may weigh more than a ton. Robot carts collect the rolls from the warehouse and carry them to the printing plant. The robots find their way around by following cables buried in the floor. A wrapper covers each roll of paper to prevent damage. To prepare the roll for printing, a de-heading machine automatically removes the wrapper from each end of the roll.

Robot carts run along wires underneath the floor.

The web enters the press at ground floor level. The first set of rollers prints both sides with the cyan (blue) portions of every color picture.

The web is now at the correct tension.

The unwrapped roll is carried to the press.

A printworker carefully removes the remainder of the paper by hand.

De-heading machine

Feeding the press

When the robot arrives at the press room, a splicing unit attaches the new roll to the web—the reel that runs through the press. A sensor detects when a roll of paper is almost empty and loads a fresh one without stopping the press. The paper winds up through the press room floor.

Photocopy

Introduced in 1949, the first photocopier was slow. Fourteen manual operations were needed to make a copy. Today's copiers use the same principles but are much quicker.

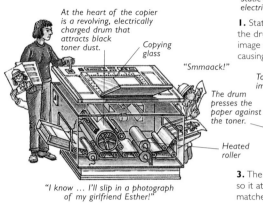

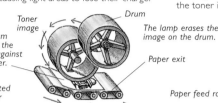

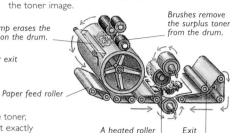

The image is projected onto the drum.

Toner deposited on the drum

Paper feeds in

Revolving drum

"Get a move on!"

"Hurry up!"

"AAARGH! WHO is that!"

"Grrr! My tie!"

At the heart of the copier is a revolving, electrically charged drum that attracts black toner dust.

Copying glass

Static electricity

1. Static electricity charges the drum's surface. Copying projects an image of the document onto the drum, causing light areas to lose their charge.

2. Dark areas stay charged and attract toner dust. Then the drum revolves, drawing in paper and pressing it against the toner image.

4. Passing the paper between a pair of heated rollers fuses (melts) the image permanently into the paper.

"Smmaack!"

The drum presses the paper against the toner.

Toner image

Drum

The lamp erases the image on the drum.

Paper exit

Brushes remove the surplus toner from the drum.

Heated roller

Paper feed roller

"I know … I'll slip in a photograph of my girlfriend Esther!"

3. The paper has an opposite charge to the toner, so it attracts the black dust in a pattern that exactly matches the dark areas of the original document.

A heated roller fuses the toner.

Exit roller

5. Today's copiers are fast and reliable, and pressing a single "print" button makes "a perfect copy every time"!

Mummy

The ancient Egyptians preserved people's bodies so their souls could inhabit them in the afterlife. The method they used, called mummification, involved removing the insides and treating the body with chemicals. Only wealthy people could be mummified because the process was very costly.

Animals were mummified, too.

1. The embalmers began by scooping out the brains through the nose using special hooks and spoons.

2. They then removed internal organs such as the heart, lungs, and liver and washed the body in spiced palm wine.

Bags of natron

Some workers washed the body.

Others packed things inside and treated the skin.

3. To dry and preserve the corpse, it was packed in natron (naturally occurring sodium carbonate).

4. After 6 weeks, embalmers washed it again and packed linen, sawdust, and mud inside. Oil and wax preserved the skin.

The more important people were, the bigger their crowd of mourners.

Canopic jar lids took the shape of human, falcon, dog, and jackal heads.

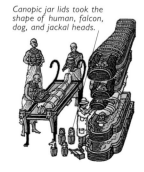

Oiling bandages

5. Twenty layers of bandage strips were carefully dipped in oil, then wound around the corpse.

6. A mask with the dead person's features went on the face. The organs were stored in special urns called canopic jars.

Underground railway tunnel

Tunnels are dug by boring machines, which are surprisingly interesting. These "moles" cut tunnels or pipelines through soft soil. Only the fastest tunneling machines dig as quickly as the common mole, which burrows 18 ft (5.5 m) an hour.

The spoil conveyor carries excavated earth from the access shaft to waiting dump trucks.

Huge fans ventilate the tunnel and supply air to the workers below the ground.

Ventilation shaft

A stairway provides access to the works below.

TBM guidance laser

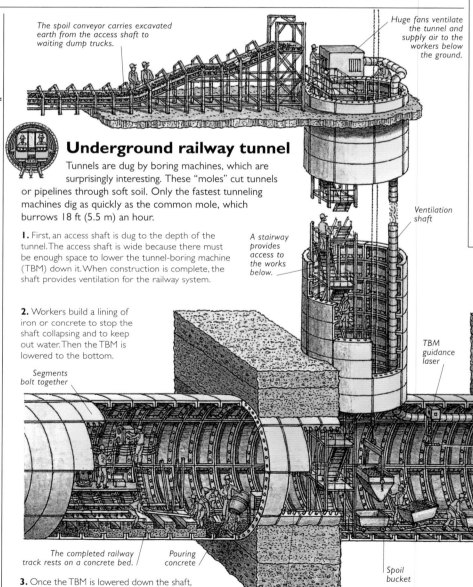

1. First, an access shaft is dug to the depth of the tunnel. The access shaft is wide because there must be enough space to lower the tunnel-boring machine (TBM) down it. When construction is complete, the shaft provides ventilation for the railway system.

2. Workers build a lining of iron or concrete to stop the shaft collapsing and to keep out water. Then the TBM is lowered to the bottom.

Segments bolt together

The completed railway track rests on a concrete bed.

Pouring concrete

Spoil bucket

Tunnel segment bolt

Base of stairway

3. Once the TBM is lowered down the shaft, workers begin to use it to dig the tunnel. Mine cars running on temporary tracks carry spoil (excavated soil) to the foot of the access shaft.

4. At the foot of the shaft, workers empty the spoil into a bucket for removal by crane. Some tunnels use conveyors to remove spoil up a sloping shaft.

5. The TBM is laser-guided. The operator knows the tunnel is straight when a laser hits the target ahead.

6. Scrapers secured to a rotating cutting wheel on the front of the TBM actually dig the tunnel. Earth falls through the wheel's "spokes" onto a conveyor belt.

Dinosaur skeleton

Scientists who excavate fossilized dinosaur bones need the muscles of a construction worker and the brains of a detective.

Bones can be hidden deep in solid rock, so a road drill and crane can be useful.

1. After recording its position, workers protect each bone with sacking and plaster.

2. Back at the laboratory, technicians remove the plaster, along with any rock.

3. Paleontologists study the bones and teeth to judge how the beast lived and moved.

4. Artists sketch details that would not show up in photographs of the bones.

Liquid resin

Pouring resin

5. Technicians make molds, then fill them with resin.

6. This forms identical but much lighter replicas of the dinosaur's bones.

7. Finally, the replica bones are assembled on an armature (steel frame). This provides an impression of the dinosaur's vast bulk, but animated models give a better idea of how the creature looked.

No paleontologist would repeat the errors of the past and mount a meat-eater's head on a vegetarian's body.

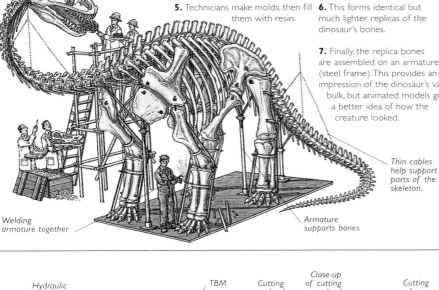

Welding armature together

Armature supports bones

Thin cables help support parts of the skeleton.

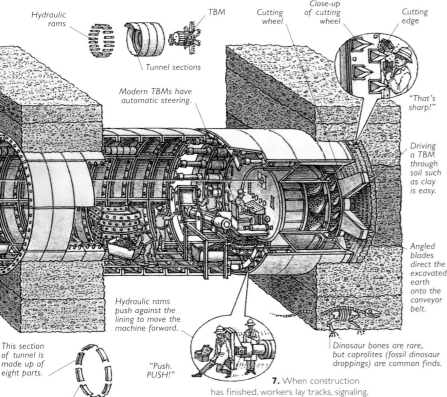

Hydraulic rams

TBM

Tunnel sections

Cutting wheel

Close-up of cutting wheel

Cutting edge

Modern TBMs have automatic steering.

"That's sharp!"

Driving a TBM through soil such as clay is easy.

Hydraulic rams push against the lining to move the machine forward.

Angled blades direct the excavated earth onto the conveyor belt.

This section of tunnel is made up of eight parts.

"Push. PUSH!"

Dinosaur bones are rare, but coprolites (fossil dinosaur droppings) are common finds.

Tunnel sections bolt together. Assembling each ring from segments takes 15–30 minutes.

7. When construction has finished, workers lay tracks, signaling, communications, and ventilation equipment. A duplicated electricity supply ensures that a power failure never leaves stations and trains in darkness.

Gas

Gas is extracted by a long drill pipe 9,200 ft (2,800 m) under the sea bed. A drill pipe this long is as bendy as an earthworm.

1. The platform drills deep holes through solid undersea rock to reach gas reserves.

2. Turning the long pipe rotates the drill bit to cut a deeper hole.

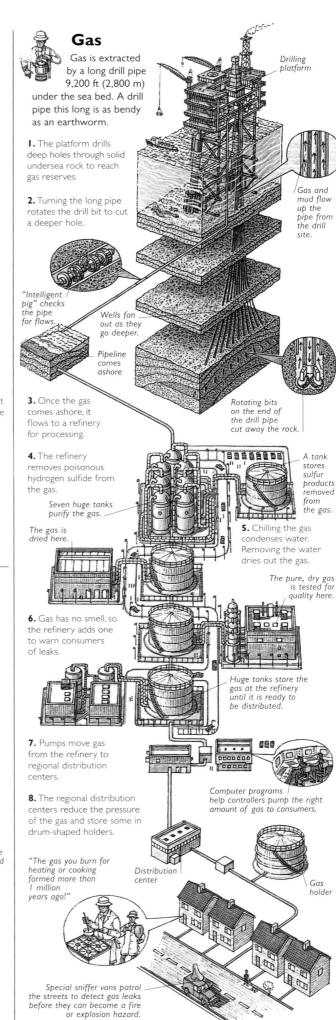

Drilling platform

Gas and mud flow up the pipe from the drill site.

"Intelligent pig" checks the pipe for flaws.

Wells fan out as they go deeper.

Pipeline comes ashore

Rotating bits on the end of the drill pipe cut away the rock.

3. Once the gas comes ashore, it flows to a refinery for processing.

4. The refinery removes poisonous hydrogen sulfide from the gas.

Seven huge tanks purify the gas.

The gas is dried here.

A tank stores sulfur products removed from the gas.

5. Chilling the gas condenses water. Removing the water dries out the gas.

The pure, dry gas is tested for quality here.

6. Gas has no smell, so the refinery adds one to warn consumers of leaks.

Huge tanks store the gas at the refinery until it is ready to be distributed.

7. Pumps move gas from the refinery to regional distribution centers.

8. The regional distribution centers reduce the pressure of the gas and store some in drum-shaped holders.

Computer programs help controllers pump the right amount of gas to consumers.

Distribution center

Gas holder

"The gas you burn for heating or cooking formed more than 1 million years ago!"

Special sniffer vans patrol the streets to detect gas leaks before they can become a fire or explosion hazard.

INDEX

ACKNOWLEDGMENTS

Dorling Kindersley would like to thank the following
for helping with this book:

Design: Joanne Earl, Ann Cannings

Editorial: Francesca Baines, Shirin Patel, Miranda
Smith, Angela Koo, Nancy Jones, Nigel Ritchie

Index: Chris Bernstein

Research: Brian Sims at News International
Newspapers Ltd.; Man Roland Druckmaschinen;
London Brick Company; Peter Middleton at Peter ·
Middleton Associates; Kay Grinter at Kennedy Space
Center; Neil Marshall at the Humber Bridge Board;
Dunkin' Donuts; National Dairy Council; Dara
McDonough at Disctronics Europe Ltd.; De Beers;
Jack Ogden at the National Association of Goldsmiths;
Kevin Crowley at Rexam Foil and Paper Ltd.; Gordon
Grieve at Wig Creations; Alistair Watkins, Federation
Internationale de l' Automobile; and Hugh Robertson
at the London Transport Museum.